DUDLEY W. R. BAHLMAN

THE MORAL REVOLUTION

OF 1688

ARCHON BOOKS
1968

© 1957 by Yale University Press, Inc.
Reprinted 1968 by permission of Yale University Press
in an unaltered and unabridged edition

[The Wallace Notestein Essays, No. 2]

SBN: 208 00494 7
Library of Congress Catalog Card Number: 68-8010
Printed in the United States of America

Preface

THE REVOLUTION of 1688 has usually been described
by historians in political and constitutional terms; James
II, William, and a host of men in high places have been the
leading characters; and the core of works dealing with this
segment of the history of England has been the great legisla-
tive acts and political and military events. That is as it should
be. In the present book I have intended not to supplant this
traditional treatment of the revolution and its aftermath but
simply to add to it, to introduce an element, a very important
element in the eyes of contemporaries, which has been either
overlooked or minimized in most accounts of the years after
1688. The attempt to reform English manners and morals,
though it did not enhance the glorious, respectable, or even
sensible character of the settlement following the revolution,
is a vital aspect of that settlement.

In this book the societies for reformation of manners take
the center of the stage. Since G. V. Portus wrote about them
almost fifty years ago, they have received little attention.
These societies deserve to be remembered in spite of their
apparent failure; they played a considerable role in English
life for twenty years after the revolution, and around them
grew up a great number of cooperating and sometimes com-
peting agencies working for moral reform. This book concerns
itself with the work of the societies and individual men who
saw moral improvement as a necessary companion of political
improvement.

By centering attention on the efforts to reform the moral
life of England, one may provide an unusual view of the
more familiar landmarks. In addition such a study affords a

glimpse of that process which made Halévy call England a
nation of puritans. Here one sees the expansion of certain
puritan attitudes—debased in many ways—beyond the limits
of any sect or group of sects. Here also we look upon an
important chapter in the development of voluntary societies—
those peculiarly middle-class, perhaps peculiarly English,
bodies. Finally one may see some interesting examples of the
blending of the 17th and 18th centuries in the realm of ideas,
a process described so well by Paul Hazard. In the various
efforts to improve the morals of Englishmen one may recog-
nize curious and often unsuccessful mixtures of old and new
ideas as the reformers deck Superstition in the garments of
Reason and give religious principles the additional sanctity
of political or national expediency.

In the preparation of this book I have received wise advice
from Lewis P. Curtis, who first suggested the subject to me.
His criticisms have been invaluable. I am grateful also to
Wallace Notestein for reading the manuscript and offering
suggestions based on his great knowledge of 17th century
England. On some points I have been stubborn; it is therefore
not simply tradition that leads me to add that I alone am
responsible for what is written hereafter.

In my research I have incurred a debt to a host of helpful
learned men and women on the staffs of the Yale Library, the
British Museum, the Bodleian, and Dr. Williams's Library.
Colonel William LeHardy, the County Archivist, and his staff
at the Middlesex County Record Office and P. E. Jones,
Deputy Keeper of the records of the City of London, were
of the greatest aid to me, as was Miss Irene Churchill, the
Assistant Librarian at the library of Lambeth Palace. During
the weeks I spent working through the records of the Society
for Promoting Christian Knowledge, Canon L. E. Parsons and
Messrs. Bourne and Stacy were unfailing in their courtesy and
assistance. Through correspondence with C. B. Freeman of

University College, Hull, I learned of the valuable typescript bibliography dealing with the societies for reformation of manners compiled by D. M. Davies in 1938 and deposited in the library of University College, London. James Ross of the City Library, Bristol, and N. B. White of Marsh's Library, Dublin, also supplied me with useful bibliographical information. To all these and to many others at Yale and elsewhere who gave me their advice and encouragement I owe a full measure of gratitude.

In the quotations I have modified the punctuation and spelling and the more extreme vagaries of capitalization. The repositories of the MSS cited in the notes have been abbreviated as follows: LRO (City of London Records Office), MRO (Middlesex County Record Office), SPCK (Society for Promoting Christian Knowledge). The Wanley MSS are in the possession of the SPCK; the Rawlinson MSS are at the Bodleian Library.

D.W.R.B.

New Haven, Connecticut
January 1957

Contents

CHAPTER ONE

The Necessity of Reform

IN 1698 Daniel Defoe wrote that "immorality is without doubt the present reigning distemper of the nation." [1] He was not alone in thinking England thoroughly debauched. In the years following the revolution there were voices from all sides proclaiming that vice had triumphed in the land. "All men agree that atheism and profaneness never got such an high ascendant as at this day. A thick gloominess hath overspread our horizon and our light looks like the evening of the world." [2] From pulpits came a stream of warning and complaint—perhaps, as Swift remarked, "but a form of speech"; yet he believed that if a fair comparison were made with other countries and other times, it would be found that the English nation was in fact "extremely corrupted in religion and morals." [3]

Wicked men, it seemed, were busy in all parts of the kingdom spreading their vicious creed. They were so successful that "vice was become fashionable and brave; they gloried in their shame, and men began to take more pains to conceal their virtue and religion than their vices and profaneness." [4]

1. *The Poor Man's Plea* (London, 1698), p. 2.
2. *Proposals for a National Reformation of Manners* (London, 1694), preface.
3. "A Project for the Advancement of Religion" (1708), in *Works*, ed. Temple Scott (London, 1897–1922), 3, 29.
4. William Tong, *A Sermon Preached . . . before the Societies for Reformation* (London, 1704), pp. 21–2. Tong is referring to the situation in 1690. See also Richard Willis, *A Sermon Preached . . . to the Societies for Reformation of Manners* (London, 1704), p. 18.

Richard Steele accused his contemporaries of toadying to this fashion and affecting "faults and imperfections of which they are innocent." [5] In 1691 the justices of Buckinghamshire and the London Court of Aldermen declared that the prevalent vices "have of late increased." [6] "We live in a wicked world," said Richard Lapthorne in 1690,[7] and John Dunton in 1696 wrote of "this debauched age." [8] "But at this present [1701]," said Edward Stephens, "both the government is fallen into great decay, and the people become so degenerate that they are like to become the scorn and odium of all the rest of mankind. . . . The whole nation has seemed to me for some time as under an enchantment." [9]

Looking about them at the nation and especially at London, the men who were disturbed by the seeming triumph of wickedness did not agree that one particular vice prevailed over the others: each saw a different form of wickedness at the root of the other evils. Excessive drinking was one of Defoe's chief concerns—so epidemic and widespread among all classes, he said, that the young could hardly think it a crime. Drunkenness, he feared, would come to be "the nation's character." [10] This was indeed a period of laxness in the control of public houses. Their number seemed limitless, and after 1690—when in order to cut out the importation of French brandy the distilling of spirits was virtually free of any duty—dram shops sprang up everywhere and gin started to become the na-

5. *The Tatler*, No. 77, October 6, 1709.

6. William LeHardy, ed., *County of Buckingham. Calendar to the Sessions Records* (Aylesbury, 1933–39), *1*, 403; *2*, 350–1. Order of the London Court of Aldermen, August 6, 1691: London Records Office (LRO), Repertory 95, fol. 321b.

7. Russell J. Kerr and I. C. Duncan, eds., *The Portledge Papers* (London, 1928), p. 27.

8. *The Night-Walker* (London, 1696–97), preface.

9. *The Corruption and Impiety of the Common Members of the Late House of Commons* (London? 1701), p. 1.

10. *Reformation of Manners, a Satyr* (London? 1702), p. 35.

tional drink.[11] These multiplying taverns and coffeehouses rang with blasphemous oaths and were an encouragement to lewdness.[12]

The great numbers of men and women with wheelbarrows, ostensibly selling fruits and nuts but actually carrying dice, peddling licentious books, or singing obscene ballads, worried the justices of Middlesex. These peddlers drew together large crowds, made the pickpocket's work easy, caused riots, and corrupted youth.[13] One vile book, a Bedfordshire minister complained, would send more souls to hell than all the religious pamphlets streaming from the press could possibly reclaim: "This business must be stopped." [14]

Prostitution and gambling were two more vices that attracted the attention of reformers. John Dunton said that whores plied the streets of London as thickly as boats on the Thames, and just as openly.[15] With the increasing number of these women there occurred a corresponding increase in the number of quacks advertising a cure for venereal diseases. It was impossible, according to Dunton, to walk in the London streets without being accosted by the porter of one of these imposters attempting to force a handbill on the passerby. This shameful publicity would lead strangers to give up the terms "French pox" and "Neapolitan disease" and adopt in their stead "English pox" and "London disease." Londoners themselves had anticipated this "national disgrace" by speak-

11. Sidney and Beatrice Webb, *The History of Liquor Licensing* (London, 1903), pp. 15–48. Thomas Green, *A Sermon Preached to the Societies for Reformation of Manners* (London, 1727), p. 29.
12. Swift, "An Argument to Prove That the Abolishing of Christianity in England May, as Things Stand, Be Attended with Some Inconveniences," in *Works*, ed. Scott, 3, 8.
13. Middlesex Record Office (MRO), Sessions Book 575, fols. 46–7.
14. Society for Promoting Christian Knowledge (SPCK), Original Letter No. 91, April 27, 1700.
15. *The Night-Walker*, No. 2, p. 13.

ing commonly of the "Covent Garden gout"; [16] Covent Garden and Drury Lane were the centers of the trulls' operations, and the reformers gave the impression that every dwelling in that area was a bawdy house, or at best a gaming house. In 1704 John Dennis argued that gaming had done more mischief in England within the last five years than the stage had done in fifty.[17] By 1722 another author estimated that in the last two years the gaming houses in Covent Garden alone had increased from three to thirty and that the gamblers had joined forces so effectively that the law could not touch them.[18]

Alarming as the rapid growth of these vices might be, it was not so alarming as the introduction of new forms of wickedness. Drinking, whoring, gambling, and blasphemy were as old as sin itself. They had a long native tradition. To some reformers the most dangerous aspect of the debauchery of their age was the importation of foreign innovations. Thomas Bray sounded the warning against an abominable host approaching England's shores: "the sodomites are invading our land." [19] Sodomy was a sin "that till of late rarely appeared in our histories or records" [20] and then only "among monsters and prodigies." [21] But now it was being "transplanted from hotter climates to our more temperate country." [22] John Dennis, in his defense of the stage, did not try to excuse the lewdness of plays, but he believed that if such lewdness could be

16. Ibid., No. 6, p. 2.
17. *The Person of Quality's Answer to Mr. Collier's Letter* (London, 1704), p. 29.
18. *An Account of the Endeavours to Suppress Gaming Houses* (London, 1722), pp. 12–13.
19. *For God or for Satan* (London, 1709), p. 30.
20. Sir John Gonson, *The Second Charge . . . to the Grand Jury of . . . Westminster* (London, 1728), p. 39.
21. Richard Smalbroke, *Reformation Necessary to Prevent Our Ruin* (London, 1728), p. 21.
22. Ibid., p. 21.

justified, it would be on the grounds of its being a deterrent to the crime of sodomy, "the like of which was never heard of in Great Britain before." [23]

The masquerade was considered to be another innovation in spite of its having been one of the popular forms of diversion at Whitehall in the reign of Charles II. In his time a masquerade was a luxury usually confined to the court, but the evil nature of the amusement was widely assumed. It was even rumored that the devil himself had attended on one occasion.[24] What was new about masquerades in Queen Anne's time was that they were now public entertainments. John James Heidegger, an expert at staging spectacular and public entertainments who came to England from the Continent in 1708, was responsible for their revival. According to a virtuous correspondent of the *Spectator,* this amusement was "wonderfully contrived for the advancement of cuckoldom." [25] High and low could attend, the duchess and the streetwalker. Here was a perfect occasion for all the most shockingly wicked persons to cavort in anonymity, safe from censure and from the law. George I gave his approval to the recreation, and early in 1726 there was a masquerade "so infamous that even some of the great patrons of that diversion were scandalized at it." [26] The bishops felt obliged to represent the danger of these notorious gatherings to the king and warn him that official support of "infamous" sports had brought on civil war in the past and might do so again.[27]

The stage, of course, was also assailed. Jeremy Collier and

23. *The Stage Defended* (London, 1726), p. 20.
24. Henry Fishwick, ed., *The Note Book of the Rev. Thomas Jolly A.D. 1671–1693* (Manchester, 1894), p. 11.
25. *The Spectator,* No. 8, March 9, 1711.
26. Historical Manuscripts Commission, *Portland MSS* (London, 1901), 7, 420.
27. Norman Sykes, *Edmund Gibson* (London, 1926), p. 190.

Arthur Bedford led the attack, and they were joined by others who believed with them that "all endeavors for a national reformation . . . would prove ineffectual without a regulation of the stage." [28] The profaneness and corruption of the age "hath been much increased by the licentiousness of the stage, where the worst examples have been placed in the best lights and recommended to imitation." [29] So said the Upper House of Convocation in 1711. To William Bisset, London's theaters were "those two famous academies of hell, those nurseries of all vice, those incorrigible brothels . . . where Satan's seat is, where he keeps his headquarters." [30] Whitelocke Bulstrode gave his opinion that "one playhouse ruins more souls than fifty churches are able to save." [31]

It is not difficult to assess the moral laxness of the stage. The plays of Farquhar, Congreve, and Vanbrugh furnish valid evidence. For the other dangers complained of by the moralists there is no sure yardstick. The picture of London in the time of William and Mary or Queen Anne was probably not so black as it was painted—the streets were not quite so filled with sluts, gamblers, thieves, pimps, and blasphemers—but good grounds for the complaints existed. Within a short time there had been a noticeable growth of open vice; there was,

28. Nahum Tate, "Proposal for Regulating of the Stage and Stage Plays, 6 February 1698/9," Lambeth Palace MS 933, fol. 57.

29. "A Representation of the Present State of Religion," *Harleian Miscellany* (London, 1809), 2, 21.

30. William Bisset, *Plain English* (London, 1704), p. 19. The two theaters operating in London at this time (March 1704) were the Drury Lane and the theater in Lincoln's Inn Fields (the Old Theater) which closed in the next year, when the Haymarket was opened. Allardyce Nicoll, *A History of the Early Eighteenth Century Drama 1700–1750* (Cambridge, England, 1929), pp. 271–2.

31. *The Charge . . . to the Grand Jury and Other Juries of the County of Middlesex . . . April 21st, 1718 at Westminster Hall* (London, 1718), p. 35.

in fact, a vogue of flouting traditional morality. To the self-consciously few virtuous men their own numbers seemed pitifully small when pitted against the great majority who seemed to encourage the overwhelming flood of wickedness. The majority seemed blind to the danger of this great tide of vice to their own souls and to the nation as a whole. The virtuous fought sin not simply to save souls, although they recognized the charity of forcing a man to be good—they fought sin for the sake of England.

"Few states," wrote Jonathan Swift in 1708, "are ruined by any defect in their institution, but generally by the corruption of manners, against which the best institution is no long security, and without which a very ill one may subsist and flourish." [32] Virtue, therefore, is the keystone of a nation's constitution: " 'Tis righteousness that establishes a kingdom and exalteth a nation." [33] And by the same token, "a general dissoluteness of manners in any community tends to its destruction." [34] Nothing is so dangerous to a state as "vice unpunished and prevailing." [35] While this applied to any state, it was a truth that Englishmen in particular should not forget, for God had shown Englishmen His care for them by many special mercies and deliverances. He had proclaimed to the world "that we are a nation of His peculiar love and protection, the vineyard which His own right hand hath planted . . . His Jedidiah, His Hepthiziba and Beula [sic], the signet on His right hand." [36] Wicked Englishmen were in fact all traitors to

32. "The Sentiments of a Church of England Man," in *Works*, ed. Scott, 3, 65.
33. Robert Drew, *A Sermon Preached to the Societies for Reformation of Manners* (London, 1735), p. 11.
34. Sir John Gonson, *The Third Charge . . . to the Grand Jury . . . of Westminster* (London, 1728), p. 20.
35. John Disney, *A View of Ancient Laws against Immorality and Profaneness* (Cambridge, England, 1729), p. 324.
36. *Proposals for a National Reformation of Manners*, pp. 2–3.

their king.[37] The great numbers of evil men who reveled openly in their vice were a national danger. A society permitting such wickedness to continue "will be divided within itself, weakened by an infinite variety of domestic evils, and become an easy prey to every invader from without." [38]

It seemed natural to these critics to blame England's enemies. "We have reason to believe this deluge of profaneness that had overspread the nation did not merely proceed from the incogitancy of men's minds and the impetuosity of their lusts, but that there was a most pernicious design at the bottom of it, formed and fomented by Rome and France, to prepare the way for popery and tyranny." [39] Charles II, according to John Dunton, had planted the vicious seeds now flowering. Charles and his brother had been willing to sacrifice England's glory to their own "impure pleasures." [40] The men who had shared their exile brought back with them "the very dregs and scum of that debauchery which super-abounded in those lands where they had fled during the Interregnum." [41] Now Charles and James were gone, but vice remained and was fed from abroad. It was Stuart vice, Jacobite vice, Popish vice, French vice. During the war with France one minister warned his congregation against those men who were traitors and hence enemies of a reformation of manners. With Louis victorious, he said, "they know claret will be cheap, French whores will

37. St. George Ash, *A Sermon Preached to the Societies for Reformation of Manners* (London, 1717), p. 31.

38. Francis Hare, *A Sermon Preached to the Societies for Reformation of Manners* (London, 1731), p. 4. See also Matthew Heynes, *A Sermon for Reformation of Manners* (London, 1701), pp. 7, 28.

39. William Tong, *A Sermon Preached . . . before the Societies for Reformation*, p. 24.

40. *The Night-Walker*, dedication.

41. Defoe, *The Christianity of the High-Church Consider'd* (London, 1704), p. 9.

abound (which will sink the price), and he'll give them leave to be as wicked as they please." [42] Bishop Gibson believed that the French ambassador in Queen Anne's time had introduced the masquerade in order to enfeeble the nation by licentiousness and effeminacy, which he thought these entertainments encouraged. [43]

The papacy, the reformers thought, was ever watchful of a chance to regain its power in England and viewed the prevailing immorality as favorable to its aims. [44] Over and over the reforming pulpit and press warned of the connection between popery and vice: how those cities that had embraced popery in other countries had embraced debauchery first, [45] how it was "one of the main artifices of the Romish emissaries to promote profaneness and immorality amongst us." [46] It was too obvious to be overlooked "that the nearer any age has been approaching toward popery, the more has all manner of iniquity abounded." [47] Therefore it followed that virtuous men were true patriots and a rake was automatically a traitor to his country and an enemy of Protestantism. Every prostitute was a Jacobite and longed, as Steele's Rebecca Nettletop did, to live in a country where popery prevailed, where there were endowments for the "Incurabili" to keep them comfortably for the rest of their lives. [48]

42. William Bisset, *Plain English*, p. 55.
43. Norman Sykes, *Edmund Gibson*, p. 188.
44. "A Representation of the Present State of Religion," *Harleian Miscellany*, 2, 22.
45. *A Letter to a Bishop from a Minister of His Diocess* [sic] (London, 1691), pp. 14–15.
46. John Chappelow, *An Essay to Suppress the Prophanation of the Reverend Name of God* (London, 1721), "Epistle to the Reader," p. vi.
47. Samuel Wright, *A Sermon Preached before the Societies for Reformation of Manners* (London, 1715), p. 12.
48. John Dunton, *The Night-Walker*, No. 2, p. 18. *The Spectator*, No. 190, October 8, 1711.

To those few, "the very few good men," [49] there was no question of the connection between evil and all the forces unfriendly to the newly established government of England and its religion. Satan was the ally of France and the Roman church. Every true Englishman must be a soldier against the devil in this national war. It was even possible that God also might in effect join the alliance against England. In that possibility lay the greatest danger. He might withdraw His aid from His people, or, worse still, He might take up arms against them and bring down upon them a national judgment.

"National sins deserve national judgments." [50] Indeed, "national sins are always punished sooner or later with national judgments." [51] The Bible offered ample proof of these statements. Had not brimstone poured down on Sodom and Gomorrah, on Admah and Zeboim? There was the fate of the children of Shechem and the tribe of Benjamin. Could England expect to escape similar punishments? Twice King William warned his subjects that God might withdraw His blessings from the kingdom were immorality and profaneness not curbed. [52] Queen Anne repeated his warning in 1702, and in response to her proclamation the Middlesex justices issued an order to encourage the justices and constables in their prosecution of moral crimes. [53] The London Court of Aldermen in 1691 had declared

49. Whitelocke Bulstrode, *The Charge . . . to the Grand Jury* (London, 1718), dedication.
50. Richard Willis, *A Sermon Preached . . . to the Societies for Reformation of Manners,* p. 35.
51. Whitelocke Bulstrode, *The Third Charge . . . to the Grand-Jury and Other Juries of the County of Middlesex . . . the Fourth Day of October, 1722 at Westminster-Hall* (London, 1723), p. 4.
52. *A Proclamation for Preventing and Punishing Immorality and Prophaneness,* February 24, 1698; December 9, 1699.
53. *A Proclamation for the Encouragement of Piety and Virtue,* March 26, 1702. Order of Sessions, April 1702, MRO, Sessions Book 594, fol. 61.

itself "sensible that the severe judgments of God have usually fallen upon nations and cities persisting in such impieties" as existed in London at that time.[54]

God's judgments might take a variety of forms. Since England was even more wicked than the Jewish nation had been, all those judgments recorded in the Old Testament could be expected in more violent and more extensive ways.[55] It might be that King William, who in 1692 was about to leave England "to expose his sacred person for our safety," would pay with his life for the sins of his new kingdom.[56] But usually a more dramatic general disaster was foreseen—something similar to those two great judgments that should have been a warning, but were not, against the national degeneracy so successfully encouraged by Charles II. Plague and fire had gone unheeded. In spite of the increasing wickedness God had shown splendid mercy in preventing the worst disaster of all—the triumph of popery and slavery. By ignoring that mercy and continuing in wicked ways England would add ingratitude to her other crimes and would invite complete destruction.[57]

God, it seemed, did not wish the prophets of destruction to be called false prophets. On September 8, 1692, London and some other parts of England experienced slight earthquakes. Here was a sign. In the same period Smyrna, Jamaica, Malta, and Sicily were struck by earthquakes far more violent than London's. These foreign countries and cities, according to

54. Order of London Court of Aldermen, October 6, 1691, LRO, Repertory 95, fol. 322.

55. Fielding Dunn, *A Sermon Preach'd at St. Mary's in Kingston upon Hull before the Society for Reformation of Manners* (London, 1703), p. 9.

56. Edward Fowler, *A Vindication of an Undertaking of Certain Gentlemen* (London, 1692), p. 16.

57. William Colnett, *A Sermon Preached before the Societies for Reformation of Manners* (London, 1711), pp. 27–8. See also Josiah Woodward, *An Account of the Rise and Progress of the Religious Societies* (3d ed. London, 1701), p. 12.

Josiah Woodward, had been "ruined and swallowed up by dreadful earthquakes; whereas the same God (though mightily provoked by us) was pleased only to shake and jog us in a very gentle manner." "O Sirs," he continued, "take the gentle warning, and improve the merciful reprieve, lest His vengeance swallow us up also when He next ariseth to shake terribly the earth." [58] This earthquake was only the beginning. "The treasuries of God's wrath are not yet emptied." [59]

The great storm of November 1703 proved the point. For a week at the end of the month London and all of southern England suffered from the most destructive storm in living memory. There were times when it was impossible to venture out of doors in London. Bricks, tiles, and stones flew about with tremendous force. No harbor was safe for ships. Only four of all the vessels in the Thames managed to keep from going aground.[60] So violent was the wind that a part of the bishop's palace at Wells had been blown down and Bishop Kidder and his wife killed.[61] The storm was, according to Defoe, "the greatest, the longest in duration, the widest in extent, of all the tempests and storms that history gives any account of since the beginning of time." [62] To him every blast of the wind shouted *Reform* and every falling timber cried *Repent*.[63] Scrambling aboard the wreckage, moral reformers made the storm their own favorite example of a warning judgment. Not until the earthquakes of 1750 was there another disaster so apt for their purposes.

The storm was useful particularly to those who thought the stage the root of all evil. It happened that on the worst day of

58. Ibid., "Dedication to Magistrates and Ministers."
59. Samuel Doolittle, *A Sermon Occasioned by the Late Earthquake* (London, 1692), p. 5.
60. Defoe, *The Storm* (London, 1704), pp. 24–41.
61. E. H. Plumptre, *The Life of Thomas Ken, D.D., Bishop of Bath and Wells* (London, 1889), 2, 130.
62. *The Storm*, p. 11.
63. Defoe, *An Elegy on the Author of the True-Born Englishman* (London, 1708), p. 17.

the storm some players in London were performing *Macbeth*, and during the witches' scenes the audience was delighted with the coincidence of real thunder adding a natural wildness to the performance.[64] It was impious enough to enjoy such a violent demonstration of God's wrath, but, worse still, the same players put on *The Tempest* shortly thereafter, hoping to swell their audience by the topical appeal of the title.[65] This was a certain sign of the complete degeneracy of the theater, and the two plays came to be considered every bit as provoking and evil as the wickedest of contemporary dramas.[66] Jeremy Collier argued that the storm came entirely as a warning against the evil of the playhouse, but John Dennis pointed out the flaw in his reasoning. The storm had not confined its ravages to England. "Not only the poor inhabitants of Cologne, but the very Hamburghers and Dantzichers and all the people of the Baltic have suffered for the enormities of our English theaters." [67] This difficulty did not destroy the belief that storms, earthquakes, and other such fearful disturbances were particular warnings to God's peculiar treasure, His Englishmen. Newton's ideas of a rational, mechanical universe did not have a wide influence so early, and even in 1750 William Stukeley, a member of the Royal Society, devoted a section of his book on earthquakes to their moral causes. He put forward a natural explanation for their existence, but did not deny them "the first title to the name of warnings and judgments." [68] The fear of a divine judgment expressed by the reformers and by the proclamations of William and Anne was not lip service to an idle, popular superstition: it was a statement of fact.

64. Jeremy Collier, *Mr. Collier's Dissuasive from the Playhouse* (London, 1704), p. 15.

65. Lambeth MS 953, fol. 131.

66. Arthur Bedford, *Serious Reflections on the Scandalous Abuse and Effects of the Stage* (Bristol, 1705), pp. 17–18.

67. *The Person of Quality's Answer to Mr. Collier's Letter*, pp. 2–3.

68. *The Philosophy of Earthquakes* (London, 1750), Pt. I, p. 42.

If England was so debauched, why had she been spared the fate of Sodom? The "few good men" took the credit for the temporary reprieve.[69] It was their role to save England as Jonah had saved Nineveh. The nation was still evil, but it was believed that God would not cast off any people "whilst they were taking some steps towards reformation."[70]

In consequence of all this a tremendous enthusiasm for a reformation of morals broke forth in the years after 1689. It was not the enthusiasm of clergymen alone, nor was it confined to any sect. The king, Parliament, the justices, and the bishops and clergy all agreed that something must be done. Pious laymen were willing to help in the improvement, and there were others, not necessarily pious, who for the good of the state felt that the cause of reformation was worthy and necessary. To the optimists it seemed that for a few years the whole nation was astir with a gigantic effort to reform itself. The phrase "reformation of manners" appeared everywhere.

All the means for accomplishing a reformation appeared to be at hand. A host of statutes existed under which an offender against the moral law could be prosecuted. The author of *An Account of the Societies for Reformation of Manners,* published in 1699, included a list of some of the pertinent statutes as a ready reference for reformers. He cited twelve laws against the profanation of the Lord's day, six against drunkenness, five against swearing and cursing, one against blasphemy, eight against lewd and disorderly practices, and three against gaming. Most of the laws existed before 1688. Some of them dated from Henry VII's reign.[71] The laws against cursing, swearing, and blasphemy being weak, Parliament passed two new ones

69. John Sheffield, *A Sermon Preach'd to the Societies for Reformation of Manners* (London, 1705), p. 46.

70. William Tong, *A Sermon Preached . . . before the Societies for Reformation,* pp. 39–40.

71. For a full list of the pertinent statutes see Garnet V. Portus, *Caritas anglicana* (London, 1912), pp. 240–2.

during William's reign in order to strengthen the hand of reforming constables and justices.[72] Some were still not satisfied
with the existing laws, but no one could complain of a lack of
statutes to cover most offences.[73] Nothing was needed but strict
enforcement. Hopes were high that if the king and the bishops
urged a diligent enforcement of the laws upon their inferiors,
it would be no difficult task to make "vice begin to sculk and
fly into corners. 'Twill sneak in a little time and be ashamed
to show its head. If it be not abandoned, yet 'twill no longer
be bold and daring." [74]

King William wasted no time in showing his awareness of
the national danger. In a letter dated February 13, 1689 to
the bishop of London and the two archbishops, William declared:

> We most earnestly desire and shall endeavor a general
> reformation of manners of all our subjects as being that
> which must establish our throne and secure to our people
> their religion, happiness, and peace, all which seem to be
> in great danger at this time by reason of that overflowing of
> vice which is too notorious in this as well as other neigh-
> boring nations. We therefore require you to order all the
> clergy to preach frequently against those particular sins
> and vices which are most prevailing in this realm; and that
> on every of those Lord's days on which any such sermon is
> to be preached, they do also read to their people such
> statute law or laws as are provided against blasphemy (21
> Jac. cap. 20), swearing and cursing; against perjury (5
> Eliz. cap. 9); against drunkenness (4 Jac. cap. 5; 21 Jac.
> cap. 7); and against profanation of the Lord's day (29 Car.

72. These statutes are 6 and 7 William III, c. 11; and 9 William
III, c. 35.
73. *Reasons for the Passing of the Bill for the More Effectual
Suppressing Vice and Immorality* (2d ed. London, 1699), passim.
74. *A Letter to a Bishop from a Minister of His Diocess,* p. 16.

2 cap. 7); all which statutes we have ordered to be printed together with these our letters that so they may be transmitted by you to every parish within this our realm.[75]

In this letter he also ordered each parish priest to see that his churchwardens presented all those guilty of adultery and fornication in the parish and to preach often against these sins. He commanded every minister of the Church of England "to suppress impiety and vice, and to reform all disorders as far as in you lies." [76]

In addition to letters of this sort William and Mary jointly issued a proclamation in which, after having acknowledged that their preservation and the kingdom's from popish tyranny had been a divine blessing, they warned their subjects that for this reason they resented the wickedness that abounded, and they ordered all the officers of the law to execute the laws against profaneness and vice. James II had issued a similar and even firmer proclamation,[77] and William and Mary's might be considered merely a routine form if it were not that William continued to issue such proclamations in later years.[78] Queen Anne continued the practice.[79] The crown was unquestionably in earnest about a reformation of manners. These proclamations were not copies of one another. All of them had roughly the same form and content, but each one differed from its predecessor with significant changes of wording. They were intended to have a wide influence upon the people, since they were to

75. *His Majesties Letter to the Lord Bishop of London* (London, 1689), p. 4.

76. Lambeth MS 933, fol. 15. See also Bodleian Library, Rawlinson MS D. 129, fol. 6.

77. *A Proclamation,* June 29, 1688.

78. *A Proclamation for Preventing and Punishing Immorality and Prophaneness,* February 24, 1697/8; December 9, 1699.

79. *A Proclamation for the Encouragement of Piety and Virtue and for the Preventing and Punishing of Vice, Prophaneness, and Immorality,* March 26, 1702; February 25, 1702/3; August 18, 1708.

be read four times a year from the pulpit and in the courts of law; they were also to be posted in conspicuous places around the country. A comparison of these proclamations of William and Mary and Anne with those of George I and George II makes the fact clearer. Each of the Georges issued similar proclamations shortly after his accession, but theirs were stereotypes of the earlier ones.[80]

Queen Mary earned for herself a special position as the patron of reform by writing a letter to the Middlesex justices. In effect she became the royal general at home in the battle against Satan, while William was the royal general abroad against Satan's agents. Mary wrote her letter on July 6, 1691, at the suggestion of Bishop Stillingfleet of Worcester.[81] She urged the justices to be especially diligent in prosecuting offenders against the moral laws. She reminded them that they themselves must be models of righteous conduct so that their example would encourage others to piety.[82] The justices immediately issued an order, repeating Mary's words, which was printed and posted on every church door in Middlesex.[83] One zealous reformer, Edward Stephens, pointed out that this pious letter and the justices' speedy response had brought quick results. On July 12 the forces of James in Ireland suffered a crushing defeat at Aughrim "as if the Almighty, who by his wisdom disposeth the times, seasons, and circumstances of all things, designed that very time for the engagement (which as I take it neither party then intended) to demonstrate or sig-

80. See the proclamations of January 5, 1714/5, and July 5, 1727. To carry it further see also the proclamations of June 1, 1787; February 12, 1820; June 21, 1837; and finally June 9, 1860, where the formula is cut down to its barest essentials.

81. Edward Fowler, *A Vindication of an Undertaking of Certain Gentlemen*, pp. 6–7.

82. An abstract of the Queen's letter may be found in the *Calendar of State Papers, Domestic, 1690–91* (London, 1898), pp. 437–8.

83. MRO, Sessions Book 487, fols. 78–80.

nalize His favor upon so small a beginning of a reformation." [84]
The influence of the Queen's letter moved the Middlesex justices to issue yet another order, this one directed particularly
against the profanation of the Sabbath, early in 1692.[85] And
they continued to put out similar orders in response either to
commendations or rebukes from the Queen or to proclamations
of King William and later Queen Anne.[86] Indeed Queen Anne
in her time was accorded by the reformers as lofty a position
as Queen Mary. "Blessed be God," said Isaac Watts in 1707,
"we have a Moses in the midst of us on the top of the hill, a
Queen of a manly soul upon the throne of our British Israel.
She has by her royal proclamations given order to fight with
Amalek, to oppose and suppress the armies of iniquity." [87]

Although Queen Mary's letter of July 1691 was addressed to
the justices of Middlesex, it inspired other authorities to reforming efforts. The London Court of Aldermen on August 6
issued the first of a series of orders instructing the magistrates
to do their utmost to stop the flood of vice.[88] The London
aldermen found, as had the Middlesex justices, that one or two
orders were not enough. On February 14, 1692/3, the court
sent out an order attacking negligent magistrates who, in spite
of the laws, proclamations, and orders, continued to be lax in
their enforcement of moral laws. The order urged any citizen
who found a constable neglecting his duty to bring a complaint
against him. One thousand copies of this order were printed

84. Edward Stephens, *The Beginning and Progress of a Needful
and Hopeful Reformation* (London, 1691), p. 7.

85. MRO, Sessions Book 493, fol. 57.

86. Ibid., Book 505, fols. 41–2 (May 1693); 575, fols. 46–7
(August 1700); 581, fols. 35–6 (March 1700); 593, fols. 21–3
(April 1702); 594, fols. 61–3.

87. *A Sermon Preach'd . . . to the Societies for Reformation
of Manners* (London, 1707), pp. 10–11.

88. LRO, Repertory 95, fols. 310, 318, 321b–24b. See also
Repertory 96, fols. 42–3.

and posted in public places, and a month later two thousand more copies were distributed in the same manner.[89]

The vigorous response of the Middlesex justices and the London aldermen to the queen's letter inspired certain of the justices in London to meet of their own accord once a week in order to discuss how they might accomplish the splendid aim of reformation most effectively.[90] The proclamations, orders, and letters had created among many god-fearing men a desire to help in the work of reformation. In 1690–91 these first "societies" for reformation of manners appeared in London. The apparent enthusiasm for reformation caused Robert Harley to write his father in August 1691 that "the design for outward reformation goes on vigorously." He gave as an example of the reformers' zeal the arrest of the Duke of Norfolk, who was fined five pounds for breaking the Sabbath by gambling.[91] Young Harley succumbed to the enthusiasm around him. "It is a matter for great rejoicing," he wrote, "that the attempt for the reformation of manners succeeds beyond expectation, and the city concurs so far. They have by order suppressed Bartholomew Fair for longer than three days, which is to be only for the sale of cattle &c. Thereby will be prevented a great deal of lewdness." [92]

The queen's letter stirred a justice of Middlesex, Ralph Hartley, to extraordinary and, as it happened, extralegal efforts in the cause of reformation. During the summer of 1691 Hartley began to lend his services as a justice to a zealous, reforming baronet, Sir Richard Bulkeley. Bulkeley had set up an office in Lincoln's Inn as a sort of headquarters for the war against vice in London, and with Hartley's aid he had issued orders and warrants, causing several convictions to be made in an

89. Ibid., Repertory 97, fols. 99, 137, 153, 160, 214.
90. Rawlinson MS D. 129, fols. 3–5.
91. Hist. MSS. Comm., *Portland MSS*, 3, 472.
92. Ibid., p. 471.

illegal fashion. Hartley's job in this office was to sign warrants in his capacity of justice of the peace, and this he did vigorously, but apparently without looking carefully into individual cases. Through his zeal a number of people, who, it was later discovered, had been dead for at least two years, were convicted of various crimes. Others, like the distiller Francis Askew, were convicted of exercising their trade on the Lord's day without being heard or knowing their accusers. In these cases Hartley's evidence was of the flimsiest, and the cry of injustice brought his warrants to the attention of his fellow justices in October 1691. The Middlesex justices investigated the matter and were shocked at what they found. Hartley had thrown the entire administration of the laws against immoral practices into confusion. The justices felt obliged to recall every warrant for tippling, exposing of goods for sale on the Lord's day, or any other charge involving the profanation of the Sabbath. All these warrants had to be reviewed and the illegal fines refunded. For over a month the Middlesex sessions wrestled with the problem. They found that Francis Askew had been unjustly convicted, and the silver spoon distrained from him was restored. Finally after two months the Middlesex justices reviewed all the evidence and pronounced Hartley's warrants to be "illegal, arbitrary and oppressive, and a great wrong and hardship to their Majesties' subjects against whom they were granted and that his proceedings thereupon tends [sic] very much to the endangering the public peace and common tranquillity of this county and to alienate the affections of their Majesties' good subjects from them and to render magistracy itself uneasy to the people." [93] At the same time the justices decided to petition the Lords Commissioners of the Great Seal that Hartley be removed from the commission of the peace,

93. MRO, Sessions Book 491, fols. 60–1. The preceding details of Hartley's case may be found in Books 490, fols. 52–3, 57–8; and 491, fols. 50–1, 59.

"it being the unanimous request of the whole court that the said Mr. Hartley . . . for quieting the minds of the inhabitants of this county, should be put out of the commission of the peace." [94] Hartley's name was deleted from the roll of justices in January 1692.[95]

Hartley's clumsy enthusiasm did his cause great harm. His case became notorious and formed a sound foundation for unpleasant rumors about the moral reformers. The enemies of reform could use Hartley to stigmatize the reform movement as unjust, illegal, and tyrannical. Hartley dampened the high optimism of the reformers and put them in a defensive position. Thereafter tracts and sermons advocating moral reform needed to be vindications of the reformation as well as attacks upon vice. The story got about that aside from the matter of illegal warrants Hartley and Bulkeley had set up their office for profit more than for reformation; it was informers' fees not contrite souls that they wanted. Never again were reformers free from the suspicion of seeking financial gain or of having a malicious disdain for the legal rights of Englishmen. Pious men might say that such tales sprang from their enemies who posed as reformers to discredit a good cause, but the case of Ralph Hartley weakened the argument.[96] The justices of the peace became cautious in prosecuting cases involving Sunday observance.[97] Ralph Hartley had destroyed much of the force of the queen's letter.

In spite of this setback the attempt to reform England by the action of the justices went on. The quarter sessions of many

94. MRO, Book 491, fol. 58.
95. Cf. Commission of the Peace Roll, No. 17, October 22, 1691, with Roll No. 18, January 5, 1691/2—this latter roll being the wrapper for the General Sessions of the Peace Roll, 30 May, 5 W and M, No. 1815, at the MRO. Hartley was a J.P. again by 1715 if not before. See Rawlinson MS D. 1404, fol. 10b.
96. Matthew Clarke, *A Sermon Preach'd to the Societies for Reformation* (London, 1711), p. 15.
97. MRO, Sessions Book 493, fol. 57.

counties issued pious orders. The Buckinghamshire justices were conscientious about having the latest proclamation against debauchery read at each session [98] and in 1704 found one of their colleagues guilty of profane swearing.[99] At York and in the North Riding, and in Surrey, Hertfordshire, Sussex, and Gloucester, the justices responded to the queen's letter with a suitable order.[100] If acts of Parliament and orders of justices of the peace could create a moral paradise, England would have been one by 1700.

But the creation of a moral paradise was not the work of the government alone. The Church was expected to help. Indeed the Church was an ideal agent for effecting a reformation of manners, and the national virtue was its special responsibility. It is not surprising to find a movement for the reformation of manners starting in the Church immediately after the revolution. The king in his letter to the bishop of London and the archbishops in 1689 had sought the Church's aid in improving morals.[101] "Of the Reformation of Manners Both in Ministers and People" was one of the heads proposed to the Convocation by William immediately after his accession.[102] Many bishops responded by ordering their clergy to be more strict in the performance of their duties. Bishop Stillingfleet during his visitation in Worcester instructed his clergy in the best methods of reforming manners. Make sure, he said, that a vicious man knows that he rests in a state of sin and what that means. Do that by clear preaching. Be strict in catechizing the young and take due care in instructing young people at the time of confirmation, for the best way to reform the

98. William LeHardy, *County of Buckingham. Calendar to the Sessions Records,* 2, 166, 169, 236, 249, 259–60, 278.

99. Ibid., pp. xxx, 426.

100. Edward Fowler, *A Vindication of an Undertaking of Certain Gentlemen,* p. 9.

101. *His Majesties Letter to the Lord Bishop of London.*

102. *Vox Populi* (London, 1690), p. 36.

world is to rear virtuous children. Above all, he reminded them, the clergy must reform themselves before they can hope to reform others.[103] In 1692 Bishop Patrick of Ely advised the clergy of his diocese to act in accordance with the king's letter and preach often against cursing, swearing, perjury, drunkenness, and profanation of the Lord's day until the good effects become apparent in "a hearty reformation."[104] The Church did not make the official display of enthusiasm for reformation that the Middlesex justices had in 1691. The bishops petitioned the king to encourage "the vigorous execution of the law against profanity,"[105] but not until 1699 did the Church seem to share the zeal of the justices and the various societies for reformation of manners.

By 1699 the initial enthusiasm for reformation seemed spent. But viciousness remained everywhere in evidence, and with a fast developing crisis threatening England from abroad, this continuing danger at home had to be dealt with. Early in 1698 the House of Commons petitioned William to issue another proclamation against vice, the last having been issued in 1692.[106] William's response, the proclamation of February 24, may have had some influence on reviving interest in a reformation, but it was not so effective as Archbishop Tenison's letter to the bishops of his province dated April 4, 1699. Tenison's letter took its place with Queen Mary's as one of the cardinal documents of the moral reformation. Up to the time of its publication neither archbishop had so publicly encouraged extraordinary measures for reform, but now Tenison, in effect, mobilized the clergy of his province to make a special effort

103. Edward Stillingfleet, *The Bishop of Worcester's Charge to the Clergy of His Diocese . . . September 11, 1690* (London, 1691), pp. 16–24, 41–5.
104. Simon Patrick, A *Letter of the Bishop of Ely to His Clergy* (London, 1692), pp. 4–5.
105. Hist. MSS. Comm., *Portland MSS.*, 3, 486.
106. *Commons Journal* (London, 1803), *12*, 102–3.

for the cause. He explained that he was writing because of "the sensible growth of vice and profaneness in the nation" which he feared might, unless it was curbed, "bring down the heaviest judgments of God upon us." [107] The greater part of the letter contained the usual exhortations to be a good example oneself, to preach diligently, and to be dutiful in the study of the rational grounds of Christianity. All this was quite familiar, but his fourth point was more striking. He urged his clergy to have regular neighborhood meetings in order to advise one another on methods for effecting a reform. The point caught the eye of the reformers. It seemed that the archbishop was asking his clergy to form societies for reformation of manners, and the remainder of his letter seemed to be an unequivocal approval of these societies and their methods. He advised his subordinates to turn over an obstinate sinner, one who resisted all teaching and exhortation, to the civil magistrate and to give information against him. Furthermore he urged all pious laymen to do the same.[108]

This letter set off the second great wave of enthusiasm for a reformation of manners. It was widely read and often quoted. John Wallis, the mathematician, was moved to write the archbishop of his pleasure upon seeing it.[109] Its effect on the clergy and the laity was immense. The lords justices in council called it to the attention of the departing circuit judges and ordered them to take notice of it in their charges.[110] The newly founded Society for Promoting Christian Knowledge referred to the archbishop's words in the second circular letter to their clerical correspondents and urged them to form the

107. Thomas Tenison, *His Grace the Lord Archbishop of Canterbury's Letter to the Right Reverend the Lords Bishops of His Province*, p. 1.

108. Ibid., pp. 4–5.

109. Wallis to Tenison, May 22, 1699, Lambeth MS 930, fol. 51.

110. *Calendar of State Papers, Domestic, 1699–1700*, pp. 237–8.

societies that he had recommended.[111] A minister wrote that the letter had a "great influence on the forming of the Bedfordshire societies." [112] Encouraged by the archbishop's approval, twenty-five clergymen and four justices in Lincolnshire organized a society "for the more successful discharge of our ministry, the promoting Christian knowledge, piety, and reformation of manners in our respective parishes." [113] The Dean of Bangor, Dr. Jones, wrote the SPCK that the clergy of his diocese had formed a society and "that ignorance and ill practice are the diseases of those parts; and therefore at their meetings they consider the proper means to remove both, taking the archbishop's letter into particular and minute consideration paragraph by paragraph and studying the properest way to put the king's proclamation and acts of Parliament into execution." [114] The archdeacon of Durham hoped that his bishop's efforts would earn special recognition from Tenison. The bishop had used the power he had over the civil administration of his diocese to make the officials of the city of Durham more vigilant in suppressing vice and immorality. When he swore in the new mayor, he charged him to be especially active in this matter. He obtained a list of all the public houses in order to find out which of them harbored men of scandalous reputation, and he drew up a list of pious men from whom he could choose new constables.[115]

By 1699 Archbishop Tenison had decided that the ordinary methods of the Church were not enough to meet the growing threat of vice. Admonitions, sermons, and catechizing did little good. The churchwardens, who had the power to levy fines for most moral offenses, were lax. The feeling was widespread

111. SPCK, Wanley MSS, fol. 5.
112. SPCK, Original Letter No. 22, January 2, 1699/1700.
113. Wanley MSS, fol. 145.
114. SPCK, Abstract Letter No. 109, May 23, 1700.
115. Ibid., No. 353, October 13, 1701, in British Museum, Harley MS 7190, fol. 11.

that the Church had through years of softening languor lost its authority over men's behavior. A young student of law complained to Denis Granville in 1683 that the clergymen in London had become disgracefully careless in their conduct of services: they changed the wording and order of the liturgy at will, failed to observe the rubrics, and added their own prayers, leaving out important sections even to the point of omitting the Creed from the communion service.[116] In 1693 a member of Parliament told his colleagues that "the bishops have preached themselves, printed themselves, voted themselves, and flattered themselves out of the esteem of all honest Englishmen." [117] The sharp-tongued William Bisset complained of the chancellor of his diocese who was so profane in his language that Bisset could not remain in his company. On one occasion when Bisset had badgered his churchwardens into presenting a notorious adulterer, the chancellor had frowned, said "Pish," and no more was heard of the case.[118] Naturally if the clergy and diocesan officials were to be so careless in performing their duties, there could be little hope of a reformation through the Church. But there were those who doubted that the Church even at its best could be effective. Many clergymen, inspired by the demands for a reformation, exerted themselves for the cause by writing special pamphlets against deism, swearing, and other vices. They taught the catechism diligently, read the proclamations against vice from the pulpit regularly, and kept their churchwardens busy nosing out vice. Samuel Wesley, who was one of the most active, could see no good results from his efforts. Viciousness in his Lincolnshire parish did not diminish, it increased. In three years fourteen

116. *The Remains of Denis Granville* (Durham, 1865), pp. 101–7.

117. Hist. MSS. Comm., *Portland MSS*, 3, 512. This was said in the course of an attack upon Bishop Burnet.

118. William Bisset, *The Modern Fanatick* (London, 1710), Pt. I, pp. 42–3.

people had come to an untimely end in a state of drunkenness. Wesley concluded that ordinary methods of reforming were inadequate.[119] Another clergyman sent Archbishop Tenison a paper expressing the same conviction:

> The present endeavors of reformation by suppressing pro-faneness and vice loudly demand the assistance of the clergy in this juncture.
>
> Time indeed was when the Church had discipline and could put a stop to open immoralities, but we have publicly lamented the want of that for above 150 years, and there-fore the Church, being confined to persuasives and exhorta-tions, hath lost its authority and vice is grown impudent and daring. So that if the power of the civil magistrate be not strenuously exerted, the nation must be overrun with a tor-rent of impiety.[120]

Archbishop Tenison evidently agreed. In urging his clergy to form societies he was in effect asking them to act as laymen would in the war against vice. His suggestion appalled "high-flying" clergymen who defended the traditional methods of the Church as efficient means of moral regeneration. Tenison and Low churchmen in general were willing to step down from the chancel, go out into the streets, seek out licentiousness, and act as an arm of the civil law in bringing men to a reforma-tion. Tenison and his allies admitted the Church's failure in this matter. The success of the reformation depended not on the Church but on the magistrates and the law. Clergymen could only assist them and urge their parishoners to do the same.[121]

119. W. O. B. Allen and Edmund McClure, *Two Hundred Years* (London, 1898), pp. 88–9.
120. Lambeth MS 933, fol. 34.
121. Thomas Tenison, *His Grace the Lord Archbishop of Canter-bury's Letter to the Reverend the Arch-Deacons and the Rest of the*

Yet was the magistrate more capable? Would the laws against vice be more effective than prayer? Certainly it was the belief of the throne and Parliament that they could, and many reformers agreed. John Disney, for example, urged members of grand juries and others in authority to bestir themselves. If these responsible men kept their oaths, "a general reformation of manners would be no tedious or difficult task."[122]

If you think these enormous and mischievous vices might perhaps be suppressed by softer methods than punishment, look a few years backward when the laws we have against them lay unexecuted. What reformation did the civility of letting men alone in their debaucheries and profaneness work upon them? Public exhortations from the pulpit, they had then, and private reproof, and good advice too from their friends; but you see that wickedness was too headstrong to be overruled by these good-natured methods; so that 'tis plain the authority of the laws must be called in, if ever vices be suppressed to purpose.[123]

On the other hand there were many, both friends and enemies of reform, who scorned the efficacy of the laws and the magistrates. Defoe, an earnest reformer, called the laws and proclamations "baubles and banters, the laughter of the lewd party." They "never had, as I could perceive, any influence upon the practice; nor are any of our magistrates fond or forward of putting them in execution." [124] The laws, according to Defoe, were "cobweb laws"; they caught the little flies but let

Clergy of the Diocese of St David (London, 1703), p. 10. See also Edward Young, *Piety's Address to the Magistrate* (London, 1695), pp. 22–3.

122. John Disney, *An Address to Grand Juries, Constables, and Churchwardens* (London, 1710), p. 42.

123. Ibid., p. 7.

124. Defoe, *An Essay upon Projects* (London, 1697), p. 249.

the great ones through.[125] Another critic went into greater de-
tail in explaining why the laws would not do. For a godly man
who chanced to see a drunk man or lewd woman or hear an
oath, it was no easy task to find a justice, get a warrant, give
the name of the offender, and then find a constable willing to
serve the warrant. The time that this process would inevitably
take gave ample opportunity for any alert offender to be
gone.[126] The role of a private reformer was arduous, and even
for the conscientious magistrate the enforcement of the laws
against vice was difficult. For every Ralph Hartley, Whitelocke
Bulstrode, or Sir John Gonson there were many justices who
laughed at the proclamations, drank and swore with the worst
offenders, and refused to prosecute their kind. Looking back
over the most active period of moral reform, Archbishop Wake
wrote to a foreigner that "the several acts of Parliament that
have been made to restrain blasphemy, profaneness, and heresy
(to say nothing of our ecclesiastical canons) are as strict as
one could desire, but for that very reason are the less executed,
because their penalties are esteemed too severe." [127]

But whatever the reason, the fact seemed apparent that
neither the Church nor the magistrates could bring about the
necessary reformation. All the proclamations, orders, and letters were for nothing without some radical change in the
methods of controlling vice. The problem was urgent, destruction was near. "If there be no power in the Church sufficient
to enforce a regularity of life, and the civil magistrate be remiss
and negligent, great confusions and disorder will need ensue
in that state." [128] If the revolution was to be a success, it would
have to be a moral as well as a political revolution. All the

125. Defoe, *The Poor Man's Plea*, p. 10.
126. *Shortest Way with Whores and Rogues* (London? 1703?),
pp. 47–8.
127. *Memoirs of Viscountess Sundon* (London, 1847), *1*, 84.
128. John Lacy, *A Moral Test* (London, 1704), p. 13.

acts of the revolution settlement would be in vain without the essential improvement in the moral state of the nation. It seemed that in the war against vice England had suddenly found herself without an army.

CHAPTER TWO

The Army of Reform

NEITHER the Church nor the State furnished the army of reformers. Its ranks did indeed include justices of the peace, constables, and clergymen, but the army was a private army, making its own rules, appointing its own leaders. The army was the societies for reformation of manners.

The first society for reformation was formed about 1690 in the Tower Hamlets in London's East End. Shocked by the openness of vice and by the failure of the justices and constables to cope with it, a group of men, a mere four or five by most accounts, met together to find some means of improving the morals of their neighbors.[1] All of these men were members of the Established Church "and most of them private men." [2] Their first goal was the suppression of bawdy-houses, which they considered to be the nurseries of all manner of vice and crime. Within a short time other earnest men joined with them and the group drew up a formal agreement.[3] They resolved to meet on the first Monday of each month at three in

1. This account of the founding and progress of the early societies is taken from Edward Stephens, *The Beginning and Progress of a Needful and Hopeful Reformation,* pp. 4 ff.; *An Account of the Societies for Reformation of Manners* (London, 1699), pp. 1–30; and *Proposals for a National Reformation of Manners* (London, 1694), preface.

2. Edward Fowler, *A Vindication of an Undertaking of Certain Gentlemen,* p. 6. *An Account of the Progress of the Reformation of Manners* (12th ed. London, 1704), p. 7.

3. "The Agreement of the Tower Hamlet Society," Rawlinson MS D. 129, fols. 16–27.

the afternoon "to consult . . . upon the best methods for putting the laws in execution against houses of lewdness and debauchery, and also against drunkenness, swearing and cursing, and profanation of the Lord's day." [4] A committee of nine, chosen anew each month, directed the everyday work of the society, paying out necessary funds, receiving information concerning immorality, and supervising the society's employees. It was provided that there should be two men paid by the society to seek out bawdy-houses and persons who frequented them and to initiate prosecutions against men and women guilty of cursing, swearing, and drunkenness. Once a year the society hoped to designate from its membership four or more stewards for each ward of the city of London and for each adjacent parish at least two stewards "whose business shall be to inquire into the behavior of the constables and other officers in the said parish and wards that the committee may be truly informed of those who do faithfully as to this business." [5]

There were elaborate provisions in this agreement for the keeping of business-like records. The four men chosen each year as treasurers were naturally ordered to account carefully for expenses and for contributions to the society. A clerk was to record minutes of the meetings, and the two men employed to smell out vice were to keep records of their prosecutions, giving the name of the offender, his address, his offence and punishment, together with the name of the constable who assisted in the prosecution and the justice who disposed of the case.[6] The agreement concluded with the hope that, since "the passions and contentions of men have often proved fatal to the best and most hopeful designs . . . we will endeavor . . . to

4. Ibid., fol. 16.
5. Ibid., fol. 22.
6. Some of these journals, dating from 1704–15, exist in the Rawlinson MSS D. 1396–1404. They are described in Reginald Lennard, ed., *Englishmen at Rest and Play* (Oxford, 1931), pp. 140–1.

prevent all differences and animosities . . . that matters may be carried on amongst us with all possible charity and condescension." [7]

Passions and contentions there were to be, but for the moment the idea of forming a society seemed to thrive. Shortly after this agreement was made, one of the subscribers moved from the Tower Hamlets westward to the Strand. His description of the original society led his new neighbors to form a similar group. Many of the men in this area were not permanent residents of London and could not engage in the parish work of the first society. They "thought something of a more universal nature, and such as private persons by their pains and purses might promote, more proper for them." [8] To these men the evil example of the last two reigns and the laxity of the magistrates were responsible for the prevalence of vice. Hence the first step toward a reformation must come from above. Since they were deciding on the aims and methods of their society in the summer of 1691—the summer in which Queen Mary sent her letter to the Middlesex justices—the members concluded that even if the justices were willing to issue warrants as readily as they issued their order against vice, they could do little without information. Therefore they resolved to enlist as many informers as they could; and to make the work of informing as easy as possible, they had blank warrants printed at their own expense. A member of the society, upon the word of an informer, could fill out one of these warrants and take it to a justice, who, after examining the member under oath, would sign and seal it. In order to save the justice the trouble of sending the signed warrant to the proper parish officer, the member of the society would keep it himself. Once a week an employee of the society would make the rounds of

7. Rawlinson MS D. 129, fol. 27.

8. Edward Stephens, *The Beginning and Progress of a Needful and Hopeful Reformation*, p. 4.

the society's members to collect their signed warrants and deliver them to the proper officer. Each member of the society was to keep an account of his warrants and see that the constables perform their duty in bringing an offender to justice. The members were to make lists of the constables and justices who handled their warrants, lists which could be turned into the justices at the petty sessions, so that the justices would know which officers were faithful in carrying out their duties and which were not.

To Edward Stephens this society in the Strand was the true progenitor of later societies for reformation. The Tower Hamlets society had made no conscious attempt to spread its work. It was a local society formed to solve a local problem. But the Strand society had a vision of a general reformation. It printed the Middlesex and London orders in reply to the queen's letter and sent copies to the justices of other counties, hoping that they would publish similar orders. Stephens, who later took to himself the credit of forming the society and choosing its earliest members,[9] wrote the first of a long series of books designed by their authors to encourage the formation of such societies. His book, published probably in the early months of 1692, was called *The Beginning and Progress of a Needful and Hopeful Reformation in England with the First Encounter of the Enemy against It, His Wiles Detected and His Design ('t May Be Hop'd) Defeated.* Much of the enthusiasm and hope that the queen's letter had encouraged was dashed by the discovery of Ralph Hartley's carelessness, and Stephens wrote his book not only to spread the news of the Strand society, but to defend Ralph Hartley. No novice at writing angry pamphlets, Stephens relished controversy. His

9. Edward Stephens, *A Seasonable and Necessary Admonition to the Gentlemen of the First Society for Reformation of Manners,* p. 4. For the evidence of Stephens' authorship of this book see Rawlinson MS D. 673, fol. 21.

book was a bitter assault on the Middlesex justices, whom he accused of spoiling the peaceful work of reformation by their malicious accusations against Hartley. The Middlesex Commission of the Peace, he said, was the worst in the nation, a very haven for dishonest lawyers. In spite of the order which had followed so speedily upon the queen's letter, the justices had not acted in the cause of reformation with any enthusiasm. Informers "were put off, checked, and discouraged for their pains," [10] and when John Dunton's *Athenian Mercury* intimated that justices unwilling to encourage reformation were therefore opposed to the new government of England, the justices, so Stephens said, revealed their true stripe by attempting to have the *Mercury* suppressed.[11] The sluggishness of the justices did not discourage the informers. According to Stephens, these splendid men persisted until they found a justice willing to act swiftly and allow them to return to their trades. The justice they found was Ralph Hartley. Since he alone was cooperative, he was deluged with warrants. This "sober, virtuous, and generous person" [12] had acted to the best of his ability. To be sure, in the rush of business he had made some mistakes, but they were all reasonable mistakes, and the findings of the committee of justices were a calumny against him. Stephens denied that there was any basis for the charge that an office existed in Lincoln's Inn, set up to supervise the work of the justices. He alleged that the committee of justices had included in their report the opinion "that the multiplicity of those irregular convictions is a great hindrance to their Majesties' revenue of excise, and a great oppression upon the people and tends to the ruin of most victuallers and alehouse-keepers and makes the present government uneasy to them as appears

10. Edward Stephens, *Beginning and Progress*, p. 14.
11. Ibid., pp. 14–15. See "Athenian Mercury," *Athenian Gazette*, 3, No. 12 (September 5, 1691).
12. Edward Stephens, *Beginning and Progress*, p. 16.

to us by their frequent and daily complaints." [13] To this Stephens uttered a righteous reply. "Oh, the loyalty and policy of the late reigns! Not yet forgotten. But they forgot we have now princes of more magnanimity and religion than to stoop to so mean policies as the augmentation of their revenue by the profanation of religion, the corruption of the manners of the people, and the violation of the laws." [14] For the concern expressed by the justices for the alehouse-keepers Stephens had nothing but sarcasm: "the profound wisdom and goodness of these gentlemen." [15] A good government it is that makes itself uneasy to wrongdoers. The justices, so Stephens said, were evil and unjust men. They were not well-disposed to any reformation of manners, which to Stephens meant that they were not well-disposed to the new rulers of England.

Stephens' book was meant to be an attack on vice, even though the Middlesex justices seemed to sustain the hardest blows. In any event his work served to publicize the Strand society and the person of Edward Stephens. According to a later account of his, he and some of his colleagues were called before the Lords Commissioners of the Great Seal to answer for the charges made in the book.[16] Far from silencing Stephens, this experience encouraged him to assault Parliament, particularly the members of the House of Commons and the bishops. "And for the House of Commons, I must declare I know no greater danger both to religion and to the government than from them." [17] The present bishops were the most "insignificant body of men upon the face of the earth." [18] In this later book even

13. Ibid., pp. 25–6. I can find no statement of this kind in the records of the Middlesex Sessions.

14. Ibid., p. 27.

15. Ibid., p. 28.

16. Edward Stephens, *A Seasonable and Necessary Admonition,* pp. 2–3.

17. Ibid., p. 7.

18. Ibid., p. 6.

the members of the reforming society are under fire. The members of the Strand society had become lukewarm in their work, and Stephens was prepared to wash his hands of them and step down from his position as their adviser and advocate. The truth is, although he had done much to spread the tidings of moral reformation, he had at the same time introduced the element of discord. The societies after his time were seldom to be free of "the passions and contentions of men" that the Tower Hamlets reformers had hoped to avoid.

Meanwhile the idea of societies for reformation was spreading through London and beyond. A group of London constables and other officers, influenced by the queen's letter, by some orders of the lord mayor, and possibly by the writings of Edward Stephens, formed a similar society. They arranged for weekly meetings to be held in an orderly and secret fashion and agreed to divide their tours of duty so as to be more effective in the enforcement of the laws against debauchery and profaneness.[19] Warned perhaps by the fate of Ralph Hartley, they submitted some questions as to the proper way of apprehending and prosecuting offenders to the former lord chief justice, Sir Francis Pemberton, who returned careful and detailed answers to each query.[20] Thus organized and instructed, the constables were in an excellent position to further the cause of reformation, having many advantages over the groups of zealous laymen.

By 1699 there were eight more groups of householders and officers working for the cause in London,[21] and by 1701 there were "near twenty societies of various qualities and functions,

19. It is possible to date the formation of this society only as sometime between the latter part of 1691 and 1697. See "An Agreement of Divers Constables and Other Officers of London," Rawlinson MS D. 129, fols. 28–31.

20. Rawlinson MS D. 129, fols. 32–5.

21. *An Account of the Societies for Reformation of Manners,* p. 14.

formed in subordination and correspondency one with another, and engaged in this Christian design in and about this city and suburbs."[22] All of these London societies were supposed to work together as a single, hierarchical organism, with men of means and position directing the actions of groups lower in the social scale.[23]

Spurred on by the royal proclamations and by the growing number of orders of the local officials, encouraged by publications of the London societies and by personal correspondence, men in the provinces copied the idea. By 1699 there were societies in Gloucester, Leicester, Coventry, Shrewsbury, Hull, and Tamworth.[24] In the Isle of Wight there was a society for reformation made up almost entirely of Anglican clergymen,[25] and in Wiltshire at Longbridge Deverill a parson formed a society consisting of elderly people.[26] Derby had a society of dissenters.[27] At Canterbury a society existed with forty members, but it was hampered in its work by the hostility of all but two justices.[28] There were two societies in Portsmouth; one consisted of the mayor, justices of the peace, and aldermen; the other, of tradesmen, in 1700 had twenty-three members.[29] Bishop Stratford of Chester thought highly of the project and went about his diocese encouraging the formation of societies. With his help societies were formed at Kendal, Warrington,

22. Josiah Woodward, *An Account of the Rise and Progress of the Religious Societies*, p. 63.

23. Matthew Henry, *A Sermon Preach'd to the Societies for Reformation of Manners* (London, 1712), pp. 36–7.

24. *An Account of the Societies for Reformation of Manners*, p. 26.

25. W. O. B. Allen and Edmund McClure, *Two Hundred Years*, pp. 81–2.

26. SPCK, Abstract Letter No. 335, August 12, 1701.

27. Ibid., No. 288, April 28, 1701.

28. Wanley MSS, fol. 160. SPCK, Abstract Letters No. 270 (April 3, 1701) and No. 290 (April 29, 1701).

29. W. O. B. Allen and Edmund McClure, *Two Hundred Years*, p. 78.

and at Chester itself.[30] There may have been one at Liverpool
in 1700, but it died out: the gentlemen of that city had to form
another one in 1724.[31] Although the Archbishop of York did
not approve of such societies, a small group was formed in
Nottingham in 1697 and within two months, much to the archbishop's surprise and chagrin, became a flourishing society.[32]
In the diocese of Carlisle the disapproval of both the archbishop and Archdeacon Nicolson could not stop the formation
of societies in the city of Carlisle, at Brampton, and Penrith.[33]
In Morpeth, Northumberland, some clergymen together with
two justices of the peace formed a society for reformation
under the auspices of the SPCK, which sent them orders and
instructions.[34] The SPCK also encouraged the formation of a
society for reformation in Carnarvonshire,[35] while the Bristol
society, a most active one, supplied some pious men in Carmarthen with information about the methods of forming a society and carrying on its work.[36] The Welshmen must have
been conscientious: less than a year later one of them wrote
that the societies in Carmarthen "have been so successful that
drunkenness, swearing, profanation of the Lord's day &c are

30. Ibid., p. 65. SPCK, Abstract Letters No. 324 (July 18, 1701)
and No. 351 (October 3, 1701). John Nichols, ed., *Letters on
Various Subjects . . . to and from William Nicolson* (London,
1809), *1*, 177.
31. *An Account of the Societies for Reformation of Manners*,
p. 26. *A Brief Account of the Nature . . . of the Societies for
Reformation of Manners* (Edinburgh, 1700), p. 16. SPCK, Abstract
Letter No. 7861, May 26, 1724.
32. Thomas Sharp, *The Life of John Sharp* (London, 1825), *1*,
171, 177.
33. Ibid., p. 187. John Nichols, *Letters on Various Subjects . . .
to and from William Nicolson, 1*, 152–3, 161. SPCK, Abstract Letter
No. 342, September 8, 1701.
34. SPCK, Original Letter No. 70, March 23, 1699/1700.
35. SPCK, Original Letter No. 10, December 14, 1699.
36. MS minutes of the Bristol Society (Bristol City Central Library), August 6, 1700.

generally suppressed and the state of religion very much mended." [37]

There were some places in England where the desire to create a reforming society existed but various obstacles stood in the way. In York there were "several sober men of the Church of England that incline to be active in putting the laws in execution against vice." But Archbishop Sharp was opposed to the idea of men associating themselves for such a purpose. Therefore men desirous of reform had to work as individuals in the cause without the benefits of a formal society. "Poor York! The second city in the kingdom and likely to be the last in reformation; but better late than never." [38] In Exeter also, since the bishop was opposed to societies, would-be reformers could have no organization.[39] Although in 1700 efforts were made to form a society at Warwick, lack of enthusiasm made the founders drop the project.[40] In spite of such occasional setbacks, the societies spread far and wide, and their existence caused many pious hearts to leap with hope for the swift creation of a moral paradise in England.

The dissenting minister, Mr. Gravener, called the work of the societies "the happiest omen to the nation next to that revolution that gave you your establishment." [41] In 1689 "all good men desired not a stop only of persecution, but the advancement of a national reformation, and they had just ground for such an expectation." [42] To many Englishmen this reforma-

37. SPCK, Abstract Letter No. 299, May 19, 1701. For a list of reforming societies in England and Wales see Garnet V. Portus, *Caritas anglicana*, pp. 125–7.

38. Thomas Sharp, *The Life of John Sharp, 1,* 179–80.

39. SPCK, Abstract Letter No. 303, May 20, 1701; and also No. 125, June 30, 1700.

40. SPCK, Abstract Letter No. 162, September 11, 1700.

41. B. Gravener, *A Sermon Preach'd to the Societies for Reformation of Manners* (London, 1705), p. 54.

42. *Memoirs of the Life of Mr. Ambrose Barnes* (Durham, 1867), p. 5.

tion was the most important aspect of the revolution, since only through a reformation of manners could the revolution endure. King William's work would go for nothing, as he himself recognized in his proclamations, unless England had God's blessing, and, in order to have God's blessing, a reformation of manners was indispensable.[43] The initial burst of enthusiasm and activity after 1691 made Robert Harley believe that the reformation was succeeding beyond all expectations.[44] By 1698, when many more societies had been formed, Samuel Wesley foresaw the army of reformers growing infinitely and accomplishing a work that could only bring great rewards to the reformers themselves and to the whole nation.[45] Optimists felt that with the apparent cooperation and approval of the king and queen, many of the bishops, justices, gentry, and clergymen, both Anglican and dissenting, the societies would flourish in every part of the nation.[46] John Ryther, a nonconformist minister of Nottingham, could so far forget the natural depravity of man as to tell the local reforming society to pray "that there may be in many, very many, a reformation, the effect of conversion, that we may live to see that joyful day when profaneness, irreligion, and immorality shall be banished out of the land; and godliness, religion, and goodness shall be flourishing, spreading, prevailing, and in prospering condition everywhere." [47]

It is clear that the most enthusiastic reformers saw few difficulties in the way of a general reformation. They would have agreed with Swift, who was confident that faith and

43. *The Interest of England Consider'd* (London, 1704), p. 5.

44. Hist. MSS. Comm., *Portland MSS*, 3, 471.

45. Samuel Wesley, *A Sermon Concerning Reformation of Manners* (London, 1698), pp. 15–16.

46. *An Occasional Letter Containing Some Thoughts about a National Reformation* (London, 1698), pp. 22–3. Lambeth MS 933, fol. 34.

47. John Ryther, *A Sermon Preach'd to the Society for Reformation of Manners* (London, 1699), pp. 62–3.

morality, even from their low state, "might in a short time, and with no very great trouble, be raised to as high a perfection as numbers are capable of receiving. Indeed the method is so easy and obvious, and some present opportunities so good, that, in order to have this project reduced to practice, there seems to want nothing more than to put those in mind who, by their honor, duty, and interest, are chiefly concerned." [48]

To the Upper House of Convocation of the province of Canterbury, the formation of societies seemed to be one of the most hopeful signs of improvement in those profane times.[49] Matthew Henry was more extravagant in his vision of the benefits of reformation. "If there were a general reformation of manners in our land, what a happy turn would it give to all our affairs; what a blessed change would it produce! . . . What a security would it be against the judgments that threaten us, and what a preparative for the blessings we wait for! How would the Lord then delight to do us good, and to dwell among us." [50] But a reformation would bring about some concrete and immediate benefits. Many reformers were interested primarily in saving souls and averting a divine judgment, but at the same time they would remind their countrymen that a higher level of morality would be a social cement, an instrument of civil peace: lewd and vicious persons possessed a leveling spirit; they scorned those ideas of subordination and submission that were necessary to make the nation secure and society orderly.[51]

48. Swift, "A Project for the Advancement of Religion," *Works, 3,* 28. Swift's easy method did not involve reforming societies.

49. "A Representation of the Present State of Religion," *Harleian Miscellany, 2,* 23.

50. Matthew Henry, *A Sermon Preach'd to the Societies for Reformation of Manners,* p. 32.

51. For examples of this argument see Josiah Woodward's works on the societies throughout; the various editions of *An Account of the Progress of the Reformation of Manners;* Samuel Smith, *A Sermon Preached to the Societies for Reformation of Manners* (London, 1738), p. 18; Thomas Bray, *For God or for Satan,* p. 27.

William Bisset, whose sermon was later assailed by the members of the London societies, went so far as to say that the reformers were not trying to save the souls of wicked men at all. "They may be as secretly wicked, lewd, and worldly as they please; we won't force them (they need not fear it) to an heavenly mind, much less to Heaven against their liking. But we would oblige them (if possible) to be civil upon Earth and let their neighbors live by them a quiet and peaceful life in all godliness and honesty." [52] In 1713 John Waugh suggested to his congregation that a general reformation would be the best cure for the differences "which at present so miserably divide and distract the Kingdom." With a reformation would come an end to "that tumult and disorder, that fierce heat and party rage which appears upon all occasions." [53] Any reformer would have agreed with John Dennis that a "reformation of manners would confirm the present establishment, both in Church and State." [54] The work, he believed, was practical and patriotic. It was necessary; and the logic of its necessity was so clear that no man, unless he was in conspiracy with the devil or the French, could attack the work of the reformers.

So with a high heart and a clear conscience the members of these various societies went about their business: to reform morals by seeing that the laws against vice and immorality were enforced. The Society for Reformation of Manners at Bristol was not necessarily typical, but since it is the only society whose records have come to light, an account of its history will serve as an introduction to the methods and problems of the societies in general.

At this time Bristol was immensely prosperous, a city of merchants who grew wealthy on a flourishing overseas trade.

52. *Plain English*, p. 28.
53. John Waugh, *A Sermon Preached to the Societies for Reformation of Manners* (London, 1714), p. 28.
54. John Dennis, *The Person of Quality's Answer to Mr. Collier's Letter*, p. 29.

It is not surprising that the city was governed by merchants and had a relatively large population of dissenters.[55] But the reforming society was entirely Anglican in its membership and had the approval of the bishop.[56] On March 8, 1699/1700, fifty-five men, disturbed by the moral state of the city and the nation, gathered and resolved to organize a society. The meeting took place at the home of Sir John Duddlestone, a member of the Bristol Society of Merchants and the Governor of the Corporation of the Poor. The mayor of Bristol, John Bachelor, was one of the organizers and became the chairman of the first meeting a few days later. Most of the founders were prominent citizens and merchants of the city; many of them were aldermen and some were constables.[57] The royal proclamations and news of the London societies had encouraged these men to form their group. They agreed to meet once a week in a formal and secret way, with a salaried secretary to keep an exact account of the proceedings. One of the first acts of the society was to arrange with the local clergymen for a special sermon to be given every Sunday evening "against profaneness and immorality and for encouragement of reformation of manners." [58] Then they turned their attention to curbing immorality in Bristol more directly. They agreed to appoint some of their number to search out houses that harbored lewd people and report them to the authorities. Very soon the information gathered by these investigators started to appear in the minutes. It was reported that "great numbers of people

55. In 1717 the dissenters in Bristol were supposed to outnumber the very considerable "Low-church party." "Account of the City of Bristol, 1717," Dr. Williams's Library, MS Records of Nonconformity No. 4, fol. 147.

56. MS minutes of the Bristol society, June 3, 1701.

57. Ibid., March 8 and 12, 1699/1700; October 29, 1700. W. O. B. Allen and Edmund McClure, *Two Hundred Years*, p. 39. H. J. Wilkins, *Edward Colston* (Bristol, 1920), pp. 49–50, 57.

58. MS minutes of the Bristol society, March 19, 1699/1700; June 3, 1701.

under pretense of going to the Hot Well to drink that water
do profane the Lord's day by drinking and tippling in alehouses about the Hot Well." A committee was appointed to
cope with the situation there.[59] In August the society learned
that Mrs. Anne Williams, a sailor's wife, was "a harborer of
loose and base persons" and that John Tayler "is supposed to
live lewdly with the wife of John Stevens." Jane Cobb from
Dunster was "a woman of very ill fame and entertains lewd
men as is reported by her neighbors." [60] The secretary of the
society was ordered to pass these bits of information along
to the chief constables of the wards concerned.

More general abuses also received the society's attention.
Having the sympathy of the mayor and aldermen, the society
would petition them either to put a stop to Sunday travel or
"to prevent all manner of stage plays, music houses, lotteries,
gaming houses, and other disorderly practices that may further
profaneness and debauchery, especially during the approaching fair." [61] In the early years of the society its committees
were constantly waiting upon the mayor to complain of like
abuses. Because of the high standing of its members the
Bristol society had great influence with the local authorities.
Of the twelve members of the grand jury that sat in December
1704, four were members of the Bristol society for reformation,
and the jury's presentment was eloquent in its concern for the
growth of impiety and vice in the city.[62] Three years earlier,
in a letter to the SPCK, Arthur Bedford had boasted:

> That their society for reformation had obtained of the
> grand jury a presentment of such magistrates as live not
> in the city and of others that were uncapable of acting

59. Ibid., April 9, 1700.
60. Ibid., August 6, 1700.
61. Ibid., July 9, 1700; August 13, 1700.
62. Arthur Bedford, *Serious Reflections on the Scandalous Abuse
and Effects of the Stage*, pp. 5–6.

and had obliged them to appoint their deputies. That they visit constantly the taverns and alehouses and of the latter have suppressed one half, and particularly that the alehouses in his parish are reduced from 37 to 18. That they had detected a notorious cheat of the aleconners who were wont to procure from the apothocaries what they call grains and other intoxicating drugs, which being infused into drink causes a great thirst in those that take of it, flies into their brains and soon bereaves them of their sense and reason, and that they will take away the licences of such persons as they can find using it.[63]

Such enthusiasm for smelling out vice lasted only a short time in Bristol. By the first months of 1702 little was appearing in the minutes about prosecutions, informers, and petitions to the mayor. By that time the society, having come more and more under the influence of the SPCK, was interested chiefly in the foundation and support of charity schools. From the first the education of poor children had been a concern of the society. By 1702 it was virtually the society's sole concern. The minutes became brief records of donations to schools; attendance at the meetings fell off drastically, and the meetings took place only a few times a year. Reformation of manners in Bristol by 1705 had become a routine and tepid affair.

The Bristol society had agreed at its first meeting that the members themselves would do the work of informing against vicious persons, but it is clear from their records that, like the Tower Hamlets society and most other reforming societies, they employed informers at a fee.[64] The informer soon became the symbol of the societies. John Dunton maintained that a Robert Stephens made his living by informing for the

63. SPCK, Abstract Letter No. 365, November 29, 1701, in Harley MS 7190, fol. 14.
64. MS minutes of the Bristol society, March 8, 1699/1700; April 8, 1701. Rawlinson MS D. 129, fol. 17.

societies.[65] According to Ned Ward the rakes of London found
the plague of informers a nuisance:

> Towards this lewd spot, which in a hollow stands,
> Shy lechers steer'd, with harlots in their hands.

> .   .   .   .

> And when they came to that notorious sink
> Of vice, where sinners meet to hug and drink,
> With watchful eyes they gazed about, for fear
> Some sly reforming hireling should be near.[66]

In Buckinghamshire Thomas Bigg, a servant, informed the
justices that his master had sworn one oath. The master was
fined two shillings. In 1698 three soldiers of the Scottish
Guards informed the Buckingham justices of Thomas Brom-
ley, a carrier, who was convicted of swearing twenty oaths
on the soldiers' evidence.[67] These, of course, were not paid
informers, but they were unquestionably encouraged by the
published orders of the justices and by the example of the
societies—which an enemy called, in 1705, Societies of Informers.[68]

The word "informer" was not easily to be cleansed of its
foul associations; it had become more odious than ever since
the days of the Popish Plot. It was popularly used, as Swift
used it throughout his works, synonymously with liar and
villain. So unpopular, indeed, had informing become that it
was often dangerous to be zealous in the cause of reformation.
The Reverend Arthur Bedford, one of the most active mem-

65. John Dunton, *The Life and Errors of John Dunton* (London,
1705), pp. 334–5.
66. Edward Ward, *The Field-Spy: or the Walking Observator.
A Poem* (London, 1714), p. 16.
67. William LeHardy, *County of Buckingham. Calendar to the
Sessions Records*, 2, 67, 109.
68. Isaac Sharpe, *Plain English Made Plainer* (London, 1704),
p. 10.

bers of the Bristol society, was made aware of some hazards of the work when he informed against a Bristol alderman for the crime of profane swearing. The alderman was convicted, but he hurt Bedford's reputation by going around accusing Bedford of being a perjurer as well as a common informer.[69] According to one minister there were many cases of informers being beaten and wounded at the very door of the magistrate's house, and when they sought redress through the law, they were met only with scoffs and jeers from the justices.[70] One member of a society informed against a soldier for swearing and received this note: "Thou immortal informing dog, thy days are numbered; I'll surely be the death of thee." [71] A London constable was assaulted by several men when he tried to enforce the order of the court of aldermen concerning the strict observance of the Sabbath.[72] Another constable, Mr. John Cooper, "a zealous reforming officer," was killed by rioters at May Fair, becoming thereby one of the martyrs of the societies.[73]

Hazardous and unpleasant though it was, informing appeared to be necessary for accomplishing the purposes of the societies; therefore the role of the informer was urged on earnest men. The Middlesex justices reminded the inhabitants of the county in 1691 that it was "the common duty of all good subjects to endeavor by timely and impartial information" to

69. MS minutes of the Bristol society, May 14, 1700.
70. Thomas Jekill, *A Sermon Preach'd . . . before the Societies for Reformation of Manners* (London,1698), "Epistle Dedicatory," p. iv.
71. William Bisset, *Plain English*, p. 37.
72. LRO, Repertory 95, fol. 354.
73. Josiah Woodward, *A Sermon Preach'd . . . at the Funeral of Mr. John Cooper* (London, 1702), passim. See also William Tong, *A Sermon Preached . . . before the Societies for Reformation*, p. 14, and B. Gravener, *A Sermon Preach'd to the Societies for Reformation of Manners*, p. 17.

put the laws against vice into execution.[74] The London Court of Aldermen ordered "all good citizens" to report to the court any constable or other officer who refused to receive and act upon information given them.[75] A few London justices went so far as to promise to protect the informer by not allowing the accused to see his face or learn his name.[76] Queen Anne explicitly ordered all her officials to give aid to those who informed against immorality,[77] and Archbishop Tenison urged his clergy to inform against vicious men to the civil magistrate if exhortations and ecclesiastical censures failed. In the matter of reformation of manners, he said, the name of informer was not odious.[78]

Reforming ministers and laymen wrote constantly about the necessity of informing and encouraged it as something noble, something that Christ himself had commanded.[79] They admitted that "the informers against dissenters were counted scandalous fellows, yet none can inform against whores and rogues but will have the thanks of all good men." [80] Indeed these informers were glorious. In a rousing sermon Thomas Bray hoped to increase their numbers:

74. MRO, Sessions Book 487, fol. 80.
75. LRO, Repertory 97, fol. 160.
76. Rawlinson MS D. 129, fols. 3–8. Edward Fowler, *A Vindication of an Undertaking of Certain Gentlemen*, p. 9.
77. *A Proclamation for the Encouragement of Piety and Virtue*, August 18, 1708.
78. *His Grace the Lord Archbishop of Canterbury's Letter to the Right Reverend the Lords Bishops of His Province* (London, 1699), pp. 5–6.
79. For example see *A Short Vindication of Those Pious and Useful Persons* (London, 1701); *A Short Answer to the Objections That Are Made by Ill or Ignorant Men against Those Pious and Useful Persons* (London, 1701); Samuel Wesley, *A Sermon Concerning Reformation of Manners*, p. 35.
80. *Shortest Way with Whores and Rogues* (London? 1703?), p. 2.

The war [between God and Satan], you see, is universal, and there is no permission to stand neuter. . . . But how, you'll say, shall you act your proper part and in what manner and method do your duty in this general, this vastly extended war!

Why, if you find yourselves possessed of a noble and heroic spirit, if you feel in your breasts a generous ardor, if you thirst for glory, and affect the post of honor, turn informers. These are they who offer and present themselves for the grand attack; these bravely scale the walls of sin; these carry off the devil's vassals captives after them, hauling them to the tribunal of the Christian magistrates, to receive their sentence and suffer condign punishment.[81]

In order to ease the informers' tasks the pamphlet entitled *A Help to a National Reformation* included some "Prudential Rules for the Giving of Informations to the Magistrates." This section of the book urged informers to be certain that they had actually witnessed a breach of the law. Informing against drunkenness often posed some difficulties. A lurch or a stammer might be the result of drinking, or they could be the result of something quite innocent. The informer must be sure of his ground in such a case. It was hard to accuse people living in cellars of exposing their goods for sale on the Lord's day. They could too easily offer a valid excuse for having their windows open. It was far wiser to attack those above with open stalls. The book reminded informers to remember the exact words of any oath so that they could repeat it before the justice. No doubt some informers had been overly enthusiastic in their work: the pamphlet warned against any attempt to provoke a crime in order to inform against it.

Aside from giving information to the magistrate, another

81. Thomas Bray, *For God or for Satan*, pp. 23–4.

important function of the reforming societies was to influence
those in positions of authority and make them sympathetic to
the cause of reformation. But if that should prove impossible,
the societies would then work for the removal of an uncoopera-
tive justice or constable. The informers' unpopular work, no
matter how efficient, would go for nothing if officers and justices were indifferent to the dangers of moral decay. Queen
Mary, in her letter to the Middlesex justices in 1691, blamed
the alarming growth of vice on the negligent magistrates of
her father's and uncle's reigns.[82] The proclamations of William and Anne against debauchery and vice always put part
of the blame on the existence of corrupt magistrates before
1689 and after. The reformers naturally took up the cry. A
section of John Dunton's *The Night-Walker,* dedicated to the
magistrates of London and Westminster, accused those officials
of failing to do their duty.[83] Daniel Defoe wrote some of his
erratic verse on the subject:

> Ostia [London] if e'er thou wilt reform thy gates,
> 't must be another set of magistrates.[84]

Criticized from both above and below, the Middlesex justices
and the London aldermen repeatedly issued statements and
orders declaring their intention to reform themselves and their
agents. They complained of slack constables and urged good
citizens to report magistrates found wanting in zeal.[85] The reformers for their part put little stock in the righteous com-

82. MRO, Sessions Book 487, fols. 78–9. Mary's letter to the
Lords Commissioners of the Great Seal in May 1693 also mentioned
the "negligence and connivance of constables and other inferior
officers": MRO, Sessions Book 505, fol. 41.
83. John Dunton, *The Night-Walker,* No. 6, "Epistle Dedicatory."
84. Defoe, *Reformation of Manners, a Satyr,* p. 15.
85. MRO, Sessions Books 487, fol. 80; 493, fols. 58–9; 575, fol.
46; 581, fol. 35; 593, fols. 22–3; 594, fol. 62. LRO, Repertory 95,
fols. 321–2; Repertory 97, fol. 153.

plaints of the justices. The same justices that appeared to be the greatest patrons of reformation in writing the complaints would do nothing to ease the informer's task and would send him away with a frown.[86]

From all over England came the plea for more zealous magistrates. John Bradshaw of Nantwich, Cheshire, wrote that he would "be glad to join with any worthy men for the suppressing of vice and promoting of virtue and religion, but first we must have more religious magistrates." [87] "We have two in our town, one good one whose name is Goldsmith, a counselor, and the other is a sorry bad one, I mean in respect of his morals, and hath not been in at the church this three years, whose pernicious example does us a great mischief." [88] From Sutton-on-the-Hill, Derbyshire, Mr. John Tatam wrote that only one justice in his neighborhood was at all sympathetic and that a reforming society of dissenters in Derby had great difficulties in its work because no justice would accept the society's warrants.[89] Mr. John Stamp of Sindlesham, Berkshire, "complains very much of the discouragements they receive from the magistrates and at least of their lukewarmness and adds that if there were but one sober justice of the peace, I myself could and would by the help of God . . . make a much further progress in this blessed work." [90]

To help individual reformers and societies spur on the magistrates, a broadside was published in 1693 listing the

86. Thomas Jekill, *A Sermon Preach'd before the Societies for Reformation of Manners,* pp. iii–iv; John Chappelow, *An Essay to Suppress the Prophanation of the Reverend Name of God,* p. v.

87. SPCK, Original Letter No. 29, February 12, 1699/1700.

88. SPCK, Original Letter No. 52, February 26, 1699/1700. Bradshaw was again the author.

89. SPCK, Abstract Letters No. 288 (April 28, 1701) and No. 301 (May 10, 1701).

90. SPCK, Abstract Letter No. 369, December 20, 1701, in Harley MS 7190, fol. 15.

penalties to which officials were subject for failing to perform
their duties.[91] Archdeacon Booth of Easington, Durham, had
one of the justices' orders against vice copied and sent it to
every minister in his jurisdiction with instructions "to have a
vigilant eye over the constables and churchwardens to see
that they put it vigorously into execution and to make information to . . . justices of the peace of all such officers as
shall be negligent in their duties." [92] The reforming society in
the city of London had considerable success in influencing the
court of aldermen. The court granted the society two freedoms
each year from 1695 until 1713 which gave two members of
the society the right to vote in local elections.[93] In 1736 the
society requested the court to appoint Francis Higginson a
constable, and the court complied.[94]

The societies went beyond local authorities in their attempt
to influence and correct those in power. Edward Stephens had
reminded the reformers that it was the right of every subject
to petition the House of Commons to improve the laws, and
he urged the reformers to petition for the betterment of the
laws under which the societies prosecuted.[95] The existing laws
against cursing and swearing were difficult to enforce, and
almost certainly it was owing to the efforts of the societies for
reformation that a new and better act against cursing and
swearing became law in 1695.[96]

91. *Penalties by Several Statutes upon Justices of the Peace,* London, 1693.
92. SPCK, Original Letter No. 96, May 3, 1700.
93. LRO, Repertory 117, fols. 275–7.
94. LRO, Repertory 140, fol. 168.
95. Edward Stephens, *A Seasonable and Necessary Admonition
to the Gentlemen of the First Society for Reformation of Manners,*
p. 8.
96. See *Commons Journal, 11,* January 29, 1694/5, and March 27,
1695. William LeHardy, *County of Buckingham. Calendar to the
Sessions Records, 2,* xxx.

Some reformers were satisfied with the work of their local authorities. The society at Carmarthen found that the justices there gave them encouragement and aid,[97] and Dr. Todd of Penrith had great success in his reforming efforts because of "the assistance and example of the magistrates." [98] But it is difficult to be sure whether the proclamations, orders in sessions, and the efforts of the reformers were really effective in encouraging justices to execute the laws against vice more efficiently than they had before 1689. The records of the Buckinghamshire Quarter Sessions show a great increase in the number of prosecutions for swearing and cursing between 1694 and 1705 as opposed to the period 1678 to 1694.[99] There is no such increase in the Hertfordshire or Lincolnshire records that have been published. But no figures derived from Quarter Sessions' records could be conclusive. The offenders whom the reformers tried to prosecute would most often appear before a single justice, who could fine or acquit the accused in a summary fashion. A justice who could be very solemn and proper in the presence of his colleagues might be, by himself, capricious and irregular in his actions. A reformer had a better chance of prosecuting successfully if he himself knew the laws and could give the justices expert advice and prodding.

It was for this reason that another important function of the societies was the publishing of helpful handbooks for reformers. At the end of the 1699 edition of the *Account of the Societies for Reformation of Manners* there were advertised an abstract of laws against profaneness and debauchery; books of blank warrants against swearing, drunkenness, profanation of the Lord's day; and a booklet of rules for giving information to magistrates. Of the many volumes of this sort the most

97. SPCK, Abstract Letter No. 140, July 22, 1700.
98. SPCK, Abstract Letter No. 154, August 22, 1700.
99. William LeHardy, *County of Buckingham. Calendar to the Sessions Records*, Vols. 1 and 2.

comprehensive and popular was *A Help to a National Reforma-tion* published in 1700. The full title reveals its contents:

> *A Help to a National Reformation. An Abstract of the Penal Laws against Prophaneness and Vice. A Form of the Warrants Issued out upon Offenders against the Said Laws. A Blank Register of Such Warrants. Prudential Rules for the Giving of Informations to the Magistrates in These Cases and a Specimen of an Agreement for the Formation of a Society for Reformation of Manners in any City, Town, or Larger Village of the Kingdom. To Which Are Added His Majesty's Proclamation for Preventing and Punishing Immorality and Prophaneness and the Late Act of Parlia-ment against Prophane Cursing and Swearing Which Are to Be Read Four Times a Year by All Ministers in Their Respective Churches and Chappels throughout the King-dom. Printed for the Ease of Magistrates and Ministers and the Direction and Encouragement of Private Persons Who, in Any Part of the Kingdom, Are Ingaged in the Glorious Work of Reformation or Are Religiously Disposed to Con-tribute Their Endeavours for the Promoting of It.*

This practical volume became the basic handbook of reformers. Two members of the SPCK, taking a tour through Kent to further reformation there, left copies of the *Help* wherever they stopped.[100] Another book that reformers circulated in the hope of quickening interest in a reformation was the annual account of the London societies. Its text remained roughly the same from year to year, including a general description of the aims and methods of the London societies and an exhortation to good men in other places to form their own societies. But at the end of the book there was always a set of figures showing the number of prosecutions over the past year and the total number of prosecutions in London since 1691. On December 1,

100. Wanley MSS, fols. 158–62.

1720, for example, the twenty-sixth annual account numbered 2,000 prosecutions in the past year and 75,270 prosecutions since 1691.[101]

In the early days of the London societies, Edward Stephens had written the most popular books describing the work of reformation. After Stephens' defection Josiah Woodward assumed his position as chief publicist of their work. Where Stephens had been outspoken and combative, Woodward was bland and pious. His books are full of assurances of the peaceful benefits of reformation. Instead of the attacks on the government and the bishops that one found in Stephens, in Woodward's books there is usually a good word for the co-operation of the justices and at worst only a veiled criticism of laxity in high places. But for the vicious and debauched, Woodward had a full quiver of sharp words. His books, under the sponsorship of the London societies, were sent far and wide in England and abroad. He was the author of *An Account of the Rise and Progress of the Religious Societies in the City of London &c and of the Endeavours for Reformation of Manners Which Have Been Made Therein,* and of the smaller reforming handbooks which had a lively market—*A Disswasive from the Sin of Drunkenness, An Earnest Persuasive to the Serious Observance of the Lord's Day, A Kind Caution to Profane Swearers,* and *A Rebuke to the Odious Sin of Uncleanness.* The London societies frequently sent books of this sort to groups in the provinces, who would have them reprinted and distributed broadcast.[102] Bishop Lloyd of Worcester had two

101. *The Six and Twentieth Account of the Progress Made . . . by the Societies for Promoting a Reformation of Manners,* London, 1721. The societies also published lists of the names of lewd persons they had prosecuted, called *Black Rolls.* There is one of these appended to most copies of *Proposals for a National Reformation of Manners.*

102. For example see MS minutes of the Bristol society, August 6, 1702; October 13, 1702.

thousand copies of *A Short Account of the Several Kinds of Societies Set Up of Late Years* . . . printed, and he distributed them on his visitations.[103] The reformers had one admonition "printed in half a sheet of paper that it may be made up in the form of a letter and directed to any persons when they are informed against, or are brought to punishment for this sin [uncleanness] by the magistrate at which times the giving or sending of it to them may be most likely to promote their reformation." [104] Shortly after 1691 the London societies had a collection of the orders of various bodies of justices against vice printed and sent several thousand of them to members of Parliament, mayors, ministers, and coffeehouses.[105]

So active were the societies in the dispersal of their books that Archbishop Sharp despaired of putting a stop to the formation of new societies. He wrote the following in a letter to Archdeacon Nicolson of Carlisle:

> The truth is, the societies of London have been so industrious in spreading their books, and the success they have had (as they say) in this way has made such a noise everywhere that the whole nation almost hath taken the alarm. And so eagerly in many places are the minds of people set upon these new methods that it may justly be doubted whether it be in the bishop's power to stifle or suppress these societies though he should use his utmost endeavors to do it.[106]

103. David Robertson, ed., *Diary of Francis Evans, Secretary to Bishop Lloyd, 1699–1706* (Oxford, 1903), p. 15. *The Short Account* was written probably by Mr. Justice John Hooke. See G. V. Portus, *Caritas anglicana*, pp. 223–8.

104. *A Short Disswasive from the Sin of Uncleanness*, London, 1701.

105. Edward Fowler, *A Vindication of an Undertaking of Certain Gentlemen*, p. 8.

106. Thomas Sharp, *The Life of John Sharp, 1*, 183. The letter is dated February 27, 1699/1700.

Since the reformers had great faith in the efficacy of the pulpit to further their aims, sermons formed a large part of their literature. Mr. Sandilands of Reading, hoping to institute a society there, first raised money to support a quarterly reformation sermon.[107] It will be remembered that one of the first acts of the Bristol society was to set up weekly sermons. In London the societies whose members were Anglicans usually met at St. Mary-le-Bow in Cheapside for what originally was a quarterly sermon but later became an annual one.[108] The dissenting societies met at Salter's Hall in Ironmonger Lane, a meeting house where until 1727 the Presbyterian divine William Tong was the preacher.[109] The sermons were preached by some of the most distinguished pulpit orators. In 1700 Gilbert Burnet and Simon Patrick, Bishop of Ely, preached to the societies at St. Mary-le-Bow. In 1705 William Wake, later the Archbishop of Canterbury, preached to them at St. Lawrence's Church, and in 1706 William Nicolson, who as Archdeacon of Carlisle had disapproved of the societies, now as Bishop of Carlisle gave them encouragement. In 1723 Edmund Gibson, the Bishop of London, gave the annual sermon. At Salter's Hall the dissenters heard Edmund Calamy in 1699, William Tong in 1703, and Matthew Henry in 1712. These sermons were published at the expense of the various societies and circulated throughout the country with the other books for reformers.

Most of the sermons followed a simple formula. There would be some appropriate text. "Am I my brother's keeper?" was a favorite.[110] The Psalms and Prophets furnished splendid texts

107. SPCK, Abstract Letter No. 1329, June 17, 1708.

108. Josiah Woodward, *An Account of the Rise and Progress of the Religious Societies*, pp. 81–2. James Paterson, *Pietas Londoniensis* (London, 1714), p. 165.

109. Dr. Williams's Library, MS "Salter's Hall Lectures, Accounts, etc., 1696–1737"; MS "Records of Nonconformity," No. 4, fol. 71.

110. Edmund Calamy in 1699 and Edward Chandler in 1724 used it. William Butler in 1722, although it was not his text, made

describing the destruction awaiting wicked peoples. From the text the preacher would move on to praise the work of the societies, often comparing the reformers to ancient martyrs and saints; he would usually bring up some of the common objections to their work and answer the objections from Scripture. In the early years the preachers were optimistic about the chances of a complete reformation, but as time went on and vice remained, they argued that without the work of the reformers vice would be far more prevalent than it was. The congregation was reminded of the danger of an angry judgment being called down upon the nation, but that they were the heroes who worked to avert such a catastrophe. A student would look in vain for theological subtleties in these sermons. They were essays in practical religion, designed, as all the reforming literature was, "not to infuse into the lower sort of people a spirit of enthusiasm, but to implant in them rational principles of religion." [111]

Usually there was nothing but the most fulsome praise for the work of reformation. The following quotation from Matthew Henry's sermon was in the accustomed vein:

> The undertaking is bold and great, and one in which the spirit of a truly Christian hero appears as much as in any thing; a catholic spirit, the spirit of one that seeks the things of Christ more than his own things; it has a direct tendency to the advancing of the honor of God, and of His Kingdom among men, and the interests of that holy religion which we make profession of, and the weakening of the devil's kingdom.[112]

---

good use of it. William Butler, *A Sermon Preached to the Societies for Reformation* (London, 1722), p. 23.

111. Samuel Smith, *A Sermon Preached to the Societies for Reformation of Manners*, p. 14.

112. Matthew Henry, *A Sermon Preach'd to the Societies for Reformation of Manners*, p. 4.

When William Bisset departed from this extravagant tone and from the whole formula of the reformation sermon in March 1704, the reformers were profoundly shocked. At the outset his sermon seemed quite ordinary. He chose his text from the ninety-fourth Psalm: "But judgment shall return unto righteousness, and all the upright in heart shall follow it." Having warned his listeners that his sermon would be longer than the usual—in its printed form, entitled *Plain English,* it runs to sixty pages—he began with the usual sentiments concerning everyone's duty to help the reformation's progress. He mentioned some of the objections to the societies, but he felt that White Kennet in his sermon had answered them. There was, however, one objection that he wished to enlarge upon, the objection that the work of the societies had proved ineffectual. Here he departed from the established course. Most preachers had cited examples of the benefits of the societies' work. Not Bisset. He thought there was some truth in the charge of failure and that the failure was owing not to the government or the magistrates, but chiefly to the societies themselves. Instead of turning informers, the members had hired informers. Instead of attacking rich and powerful sinners, they had prosecuted poor and petty ones. He hoped it was not true that the members did little aside from listening to sermons, but clearly he was not certain on that point.

This plain talking was unwelcome. Bisset thought he was jarring his audience into a renewed attack upon vice. The attack, as one might expect, was actually on him. He wrote that his sermon became the talk of the town and brought him from desirable obscurity to an unwanted fame. From all sides hard words poured down on him, but no one matched the bitterness of his hearers.[113] His sermon led others to publish in response. Isaac Sharpe, in *Plain English Made Plainer,* struck out at Bisset in a most personal way and went on to attack the socie-

113. William Bisset, *Plain English,* preface.

ties as well, calling them a "miserable congregation" of in-formers.[114] It was an unfortunate incident. The societies had asked Bisset to preach at the last minute when another man had been unable to appear. His sermon was actually full of sound advice, but it was not the advice the reformers wished to hear. It stirred up a controversy that did nothing to improve the popular opinion of the societies.

Was it true that the work of the societies was ineffective? Dr. Todd of Penrith thought he saw "a visible reformation of manners everywhere." [115] Mr. Thomas of Carmarthen said that "there are some societies for reformation of manners which have been so successful that drunkenness, swearing, profanation of the Lord's day &c are generally suppressed and the state of religion very much mended." [116] Six months after Bisset's sermon, Thomas Freke told the reformers: "Gentlemen, you have run well; God hath blessed your endeavors with unexpected success; the kingdom of the devil hath been in a tottering, declining condition from the first beginnings of your society." [117] Even Defoe, who was no friend of the societies, came to their defense when a Scotsman objected to the union with England because England was a vicious nation, incapable of being reformed even by the societies. Defoe answered that "England, bad as she is, is yet a reforming nation . . . the work of reformation has made more progress in England, from the court even to the street, than I believe any nation in the world can parallel in such a time and in such circumstances." He believed that he could fill a large book with the history of the progress and methods of the societies.[118] The Upper House

114. Isaac Sharpe, *Plain English Made Plainer*, p. 5.
115. SPCK, Abstract Letter No. 342, September 8, 1701.
116. SPCK, Abstract Letter No. 299, May 19, 1701.
117. *A Sermon Preach'd to the Societies for Reformation of Manners* (London, 1704), p. 46.
118. *A Review of the Affairs of France and All Europe*, 3, 613–14, December 26, 1706.

of Convocation in 1711 stated its belief that, "through the care of magistrates and others," some improvement had been made in the observance of the Lord's day.[119] A foreigner visiting London thought that altogether too much improvement had been made in this matter. He wrote in his diary for June 15, 1710 (New Style):

> In the afternoon to St. James's Park to see the crowds. No other diversion is allowed on Sunday, which is nowhere more strictly kept; not only is all play forbidden and public houses closed, but few even of the boats and hackney-coaches may ply. Our hostess would not even allow the strangers to play the *viol di Gamba* or the flute lest she should be punished. This is, I suppose, the only point in which one sees that the English profess to be Christians; certainly from the rest of their conduct one would not suspect it of many of them.[120]

It is possible that in the matter of Sunday observance the reformers had made some improvement. The Sunday Observance Act of 1677 was a comprehensive statute more easily enforced than the statutes against drunkenness or swearing. The records of the London reformers show that they prosecuted most often those found exercising their trades on the Sabbath.[121]

According to the societies themselves great progress was being made against all kinds of vice. Their annual accounts gave evidence of a large number of prosecutions each year. The last *Account* in 1738 recorded 101,683 prosecutions in and near London in the past 44 years.[122] But the claims of the societies are seriously open to question. As one author said:

119. "A Representation of the Present State of Religion," *Harleian Miscellany*, 2, 22.

120. J. E. B. Mayor, ed., *Cambridge under Queen Anne* (Cambridge, England, 1911), p. 353.

121. Rawlinson MSS D. 1396–1404.

122. *The Forty-Fourth Account of the Progress Made . . . by the Societies for Promoting a Reformation of Manners,* London, 1738.

"All is not gold that glitters; I believe everyone of his stories will not abide the touchstone of truth; they ha'nt the Tower stamp, are not sterling-verities." [123] Josiah Woodward wrote glowingly of the success of the societies in 1701. Because of them "the impudence of lewd women and the blasphemies of licentious tongues are manifestly abated in our streets, and the works of darkness seem to be retiring to their proper scene." [124] But the same doubting author questioned his optimism: "Is the number of whores, pimps, and pandars, bullies of all sorts . . . lessened? Are the sins of drunkenness, robbing, sacrilege &c quite out of doors? I trow not. . . . I wonder what your fast friend [Woodward] means by success." [125]

In 1701 both the Grand Jury of the city of London and the Middlesex justices remarked upon the effectiveness of the reformers' work.[126] The London Court of Aldermen in 1713 congratulated the societies on the number of their prosecutions during the past years. The court felt that the societies "have by their great care and vigilance been instrumental in preventing the growth of the most common and open vices." [127] John Dunton agreed that the societies had been extremely active in the city of London, but he thought their success had been empty—it had only led the trulls to move to Long Acre.[128] In 1708 Swift wrote that the seeming reformation had been ineffectual. "Laws against immorality have not been executed; and proclamations occasionally issued out to enforce them are wholly unregarded as things of form. Religious societies, though begun with excellent intention, and by persons of true

123. [Philalethes] *Plain Dealing* (London, 1704), p. 17.

124. Josiah Woodward, *An Account of the Rise and Progress of the Religious Societies*, p. 77.

125. [Philalethes] *Plain Dealing*, p. 17.

126. *The Proceedings of the King's Commission of the Peace and Oyer and Terminer* (June 4, 5, 1701), p. 5. MRO, Sessions Book 581, fol. 35.

127. LRO, Repertory 117, fols. 275–7.

128. John Dunton, *The Night-Walker*, No. 5, p. 1.

piety, have divided into factious clubs and grown a trade to enrich little knavish informers of the meanest rank, such as common constables and broken shopkeepers." [129] Even in 1703 a note of pessimism appeared in a sermon by William Tong, who remarked that the reformers undoubtedly found it discouraging to see that vice could still keep the field after all their efforts:

> no doubt when you first engaged in this honest and honorable design, in which you had the laws of God and Nature and the nation on your side, you promised yourselves that, by this time, you should have surmounted all your difficulties, and brought your work to a good degree of perfection; that the wickedness of the wicked would have come to an end; that gross and scandalous sins would have ceased, and offenders would have thanked you for your charitable pains and care to prevent the ruin of themselves and their families.
>
> But you find corrupt nature and long custom in sin are not so easily conquered. [130]

After 1720 the same old complaints about corrupt constables and justices were repeated. [131] It was said that any attempt at reformation of manners would be in vain, and that the societies instead of suppressing lewdness had promoted it. [132] After 1730

129. "A Project for the Advancement of Religion," *Works*, 3, 41.
130. *A Sermon Preached . . . before the Societies for Reformation*, pp. 3–4.
131. For example see *An Account of the Endeavours That Have Been Used to Suppress Gaming Houses* (London, 1722), pp. 4–6. *The Second Charge of Sir John Gonson, Knt. to the Grand Jury* (London, 1728), p. 17. *The Charge of Sr. Daniel Dolins, Kt. to the Grand Jury . . . of Middlesex* (London, 1725), pp. 24–7. LRO, Repertory 127, fols. 341–2, 352; Repertory 142, fol. 531.
132. Harry Mordaunt [probably Bernard Mandeville], *A Modest Defence of Public Stews* (London, 1740), dedication, "To the Gentlemen of the Societies," p. ii.

the descriptions of vice were as lurid as they had been before 1700. To Mr. Drew dissoluteness was on the increase, with a corresponding rise in the number of papists.[133] In 1732 Mr. Knight asserted that "overgrown wickedness walks in our streets with the air and impudence of a bold strumpet." [134] Arthur Bedford, who had been so active in Bristol, seemed to think in 1734 that conditions were worse than ever before:

> Nay, this is the only way to prevent national judgments. We all know that public sins call for public calamities; and perhaps never were sins more public and of a more crying nature. The vast number not only of ginshops, but of all other lewd and disorderly houses, the receptacles of thieves and robbers and other night practices in defiance of the zeal of some excellent magistrates to suppress them, yield us a very melancholy prospect. . . . The horrid oaths and curses, which are heard every minute of every day by those who go in the streets from the mouths of porters, coachmen, carmen, watermen, and others, calling upon God Almighty to damn their own souls and the souls of those to whom they speak, are enough to rend heaven and sink us to hell.[135]

If the statistics on the distillation of spirits are an indication, Bedford was right in thinking that the situation had worsened. In 1694 there had been 810,096 gallons distilled; in 1734, 6,074,762 gallons.[136]

133. Robert Drew, *A Sermon Preached to the Societies for Reformation of Manners*, pp. 18–19.
134. James Knight, *A Sermon Preached to the Societies for Reformation of Manners* (London, 1733), p. 7. See also Isaac Maddox, *The Love of Our Country Recommended* (London, 1737), pp. 9–10.
135. *A Sermon Preached to the Societies for Reformation of Manners* (London, 1734), pp. 17–18.
136. E. D. Bebb, *Nonconformity and Social and Economic Life* (London, 1935), p. 146.

The later sermons to the societies were full of disillusion-
ment, creating a notable contrast with the enthusiasm and hope
of the early ones. The last accounts and sermons were published in 1738. In that year those reforming societies that had
not done so before gave up their work. Their methods had
failed. But their members could console themselves with the
text from which Samuel Say had preached his sermon in
Salter's Hall in 1736: "Then I said I have labored in vain; I
have spent my strength for nought and in vain, yet surely my
judgment is with the Lord and my work with my God." [137]

137. Samuel Say, *A Sermon Preach'd to the Societies for Reformation*, London, 1736. The text is from Isaiah 49:4. According to
John Wesley in 1763, the societies disappeared because the original
members had died and those that filled their places "grew faint in
their mind and departed from the work." Wesley, *A Sermon
Preached before the Society for Reformation* (London, 1778), p. 4.
The society to which he preached was founded in 1757.

CHAPTER THREE

Failure and Success

THE REFORMATION of manners was but one aspect of a religious revival which had begun in the brief reign of James II. The threat of Roman Catholicism in that time had been a challenge to both churchmen and dissenters. Popery meant tyranny, while protestantism was the bulwark of the traditional rights and liberties of Englishmen. Therefore, one way to show a stubborn defiance of James' rule was to throng the churches and chapels of England. The wave of piety that resulted from this form of resistance did not disappear with the accession of William and Mary; it persisted and manifested itself not only in the formation of societies for reformation but in the activities of other organizations as well.

Formal groups known as religious societies had existed in England since 1678. At that time some young men of the Church of England, penetrated by a sense of sin and spiritual sorrow, met with their minister and agreed to form a society that would meet once a week. Its purpose was to quicken the faith of its members, and encourage them in prayer and in their participation in the sacraments. Inspired chiefly by the sermons of Anthony Horneck, societies of this kind spread through several London parishes and were active in a quiet way up until 1685. Although they had instituted a weekly evening lecture at St. Clement Danes and had collected money for charitable purposes, they had made little noise in the world. This fact helped them to continue during the difficult

67

years of James' reign. They took the precaution of meeting more often in a public house than in the home of a member. A few of the less zealous of their number left the societies in those years, but others took their place, and after the revolution the societies grew and flourished more vigorously than ever before. They spread beyond London and were welcomed by most clergymen, high and low alike. Josiah Woodward and others publicized their activities, but the members still worked quietly to improve their own faith and to encourage young men, more by example than by persuasion, to be confirmed in the Established Church.[1] It was one of these societies to which the Wesley brothers, Whitefield, and James Hervey belonged at Oxford, and it was to the religious societies in London and the provinces that the Wesleys carried their message in later years.[2]

According to Josiah Woodward an intimate connection existed between the religious societies and the societies for reformation. In his account it was from an amalgamation of the Tower Hamlets society and some members of a religious society that the societies for reformation arose. The impression left by the title of his *An Account of the Rise and Progress of the Religious Societies in the City of London &c and of Their Endeavours for Reformation of Manners* is that the reforming societies, if not exactly the same as the religious societies, were at least a direct outgrowth from them. In Bishop Burnet's *History of His Own Time* the societies are made to be one and the same. He asserted that after the revolution the religious so-

1. This account of the religious societies is based on the description in Josiah Woodward, *An Account of the Rise and Progress of the Religious Societies,* pp. 1–47; and G. V. Portus, *Caritas anglicana,* pp. 1–27.

2. The connection between the religious societies and methodism is discussed by Elie Halévy, "La Naissance du Méthodisme en Angleterre," *Revue de Paris,* 6 (1906), 519–39, 841–67; and by John S. Simon, *John Wesley and the Religious Societies,* London, 1921.

cieties turned to the work of informing and came to be called
societies for reformation.[3] Most historians since Burnet's time
have written of the relationship between the two societies in
much the same way, describing them as closely related and
sometimes as identical. It seems reasonable to do so. Chronol-
ogy supports the view; the religious societies were the earlier
group and might well have served as parents to the reforming
societies. There is evidence that the religious societies did to
some extent encourage the punishment of profaneness,[4] and
it is certain that the renewed energy of the religious societies
and the foundation of the reforming societies were both
products of the religious revival after 1685. But in fact the
religious societies and those for reformation of manners were
very different from one another, and the intimate connection
between them, stressed by Woodward and Burnet, was ficti-
tious. In 1702 a minister, in writing to the members of the
religious societies, said: "When I had the honor of being
called upon to preach the foregoing sermon, it was not my
good fortune to understand, or at least then to recollect, how
perfectly distinct your societies are from those for reformation." [5] He may have been confused by Woodward's book. The
religious societies in London in 1694 were composed primarily
of tradesmen and some apprentices.[6] The same sort of men
seems to have provided the membership of most reforming
societies, but the religious societies were strictly Anglican and
the reforming societies were not. The religious societies worked
internally for the improvement of their members; they worked

3. Gilbert Burnet, *History of His Own Time* (London, 1818),
3, 349–50.
4. G. V. Portus, *Caritas anglicana,* p. 194.
5. George Stanhope, *The Duty of Rebuking* (London, 1703), p.
21.
6. Rawlinson MS D. 1312, fols. 2–18. Here there is a list of
the names and occupations of 265 tradesmen in 15 religious societies.

with the Church and had the approval of most clergymen. The reforming societies worked externally. They assumed that their members were virtuous, and they existed for the supposed benefit of others. They were not within the Church; rather they were critics of Church and the State. Therefore they were essentially and fundamentally different from the religious societies; any similarities were superficial.[7]

This fact explains why it was that Mr. Samuel Shaw of Warrington, Lancashire, was able to set up a reforming society but not a religious society.[8] If the two societies were alike there would have been no such difficulty. It explains why Mr. Tomlinson of Newcastle had to write the SPCK for instructions when he wished to make a religious society into a reforming society.[9] The change was not an easy, natural step. Tomlinson was in fact trying to create an entirely different sort of organization out of an old one.

The connection between the reforming societies and the SPCK was far closer. The SPCK was another and more important product of the religious revival. It was formed in March 1698/9 by a few members of the Church of England who were disturbed by the low state of morality and the seeming inability of the Church to correct the situation. The founders were capable and influential men. There was Lord Guilford, a vigorous young man of twenty-five and the son of a distinguished father, and Sir Humphrey Mackworth, a member of Parliament and a zealous religious and political pamphleteer. Sir Humphrey possessed considerable financial ingenuity, having organized the Company of Mine Adventurers of England, which pros-

7. One later writer who stressed this essential difference was C. F. Secretan in *Memoirs of the Life and Times of the Pious Robert Nelson* (London, 1860), p. 96.

8. SPCK, Abstract Letter No. 364, November 18, 1701, in Harley MS 7190, fol. 14.

9. SPCK, Abstract Letter No. 261, March 8, 1700/1.

pered under his direction until it was found to be shockingly corrupt. Sir Humphrey apparently never tried to square his economic activities with his zeal for religion.[10] Another founder was John Hooke, an Irishman and barrister, who became a serjeant-at-law in 1700. The fourth founder was Dr. Thomas Bray, who became famous for his religious activities in the American colonies, particularly in Maryland. He was the only clergyman of the group, which included a fifth person, Colonel Maynard Colchester.

The opening paragraph of the first circular letter of the society, written in November 1699, announced its purpose and the qualifications of its founders:

> The visible decay of religion in this Kingdom with the monstrous increase of deism, profaneness, and vice has excited the zeal of several persons of the best character in the cities of London and Westminster and other parts of the nation to associate themselves in order to consult together how to put a stop to so fatal an inundation.[11]

The method of attacking vice that appealed most to these men was the Christian education of poor children in charity schools, a method that would require time. Where the reforming societies looked for a speedy conclusion to their work, the founders of the SPCK looked more to the virtue and religion of the future. For them it was the catechism learned young, rather than the informer, that was to make England secure against atheism and vice.

But the SPCK was not narrowly conceived and did not confine itself to any one method of reform. In its early years it hoped to encourage every kind of reformation and sought to

10. *DNB;* and Mary Ransome, "The Parliamentary Career of Sir Humphrey Mackworth, 1701–13," *University of Birmingham Historical Journal,* 1 (1948), pp. 232–54.
11. Wanley MSS, fol. 1.

be the great central organization directing the campaign against vice. The societies for reformation were scattered and disunited. The SPCK was one great society for reformation, encouraging the formation of local units which kept in close touch with the London headquarters. Its efforts to form local societies were strengthened by Archbishop Tenison's letter, published one month after the SPCK's founding, urging clergymen to organize societies and to consult one another as to the best means of improving morals. The SPCK publicized his suggestion and in a short time became a clearing house for information from newly formed local societies of clergymen and laymen. Through its circular letters the SPCK instructed its correspondents in the ways of forming societies, with one member to be designated as an official correspondent responsible for keeping in contact with the SPCK itself. The records of the SPCK show how quickly the country responded to the circular letters. In less than a year after the first letter, the society was carrying on a tremendous correspondence with local groups who were busy at the work of setting up charity schools and in other ways working for a reformation of manners. The early letters of the society requested information about the methods and progress of each local group. The circular letter to lay correspondents in April 1700 said in part:

> You that live in the country are more likely to know what are the proper methods to carry on this good work there than we who are at this distance and therefore we shall not pretend to give you any scheme about it. . . . We have this farther to beg of you that you would be pleased from time to time to let us know what success you meet with and if our advice may be of any service we shall be very glad to give it as occasion happens; and perhaps in some little time we shall be better able to give it than we are at present, as being likely to hear how this good work is

managed in every county of England which will enable us to judge the better of any method that be proposed.[12]

In reply to this and to letters like it the society received many requests for information and a mass of enthusiastic suggestions for a more effective reformation. The Reverend Thomas Frank of Bedfordshire sent a long list of proposals designed to improve the charity schools and to unify all the various organizations for reformation of manners.[13] One of the society's letters stirred Mr. Edward Killingworth of Northamptonshire to write a letter whose contents were noted as follows by the SPCK's secretary:

That the piously ingenious letter of the society has by copies been communicated to many divines who were very well pleased with it; that as tokens of his zeal for the same cause he has sent two papers, one to the learned deists, t'other to the unlearned infidels about the resurrection of our Saviour and the credibility of the Scriptures; that if the society thinks fit to print them he would not have them part with the propriety to any bookseller &c; that he would write an encouragement to informers if the society judge it necessary and desires to know what sermons are printed upon that subject besides Dr. Woodward's, Jekyl's, and Barton's. That the neighboring clergymen give each other book catalogues of their books instead of lending libraries; that they have sent for 100 of Bishop Williams' Catechism; that they are endeavoring to set up prayers in weekdays too much neglected; that some ministers distribute common prayer books and the letter from a minister to his parishioners . . . that anything written about common prayer, reading the Scriptures, the religiousness of an oath, con-

12. Ibid., fol. 36. The last portion of this letter, after the semicolon and beginning "and perhaps," is crossed out in this copy.
13. Ibid., fols. 22–5.

versation, observing the Lord's day, against drunkenness, would be very welcome.[14]

By October 1700 the society had discovered a way to handle careless churchwardens and could pass the method on to Archdeacon Booth of Durham. The plan was to have some zealous men do the same sort of investigation into church attendance that the churchwardens should do. These men would then inform the justices of those found to be negligent in attending Sunday services. "If the churchwardens (as usually they do) return *Omnia bene*, then may the justices instance A., B., C., and demand their opinion of such persons. By this means the churchwardens have in some places been brought to inform against all such offenders lest their negligence should be punished." [15] Archdeacon Booth, in turn, was an expert on the manner of forming clerical societies under difficult circumstances. The SPCK having heard from Mr. Lisle of Guisborough in the North Riding that he was unable to form a clerical society, advised him to seek out the Archdeacon.[16]

The founding of the SPCK, together with the encouragement of Archbishop Tenison's letter, set off the second round of enthusiasm for founding societies for reformation. The SPCK had many advantages that the reforming societies lacked. Through its efficient network of correspondents, it had gathered a great body of information upon which to base the strategy for a national war on vice. Being purely Anglican, it had the approval and aid of influential clergymen to a greater extent than the reforming societies. Therefore in its early years,

14. SPCK, Abstract Letter No. 360, November 10, 1701, in Harley MS 7190, fol. 13. Josiah Woodward preached to the societies for reformation in 1696, Thomas Jekill in 1698, Samuel Barton in 1699. John Williams was the Bishop of Chichester, 1696–1709. His *Exposition of the Church Catechism* (1689) had gone through five editions by 1695.

15. Wanley MSS, fol. 63.

16. Ibid., fols. 45–6.

when it acted as a central agency for the reforming societies as well as for its own branches, the SPCK gave invaluable help to the individual societies for reformation, putting its information at their disposal. When reformers in the diocese of Carlisle were hindered in their work by the lively disapproval of Archdeacon Nicolson, one of them wrote to the SPCK for advice and assistance.[17] Archdeacon Booth reported to the SPCK in June 1701 that there were no societies for reformation in the vicinity of Durham, but that if some of the bishops who were members of the SPCK could be prevailed upon to write the Bishop of Durham recommending the reforming societies, he could organize them within a few weeks.[18] Often it was through the SPCK that individual reformers in outlying places were put in contact with the London reforming societies.[19]

Arthur Bedford, who was one of the original and most active members of the Bristol society for reformation, became the SPCK's correspondent for that city. His letters to the society were long and numerous, filled with complaints about rampant vice in Bristol, advice about methods of reforming manners, and questions. What methods, he asked the SPCK, do the London societies for reformation use "to prevent boys from playing in the streets on the Lord's day and men from spending their time idly on the Change, in the field, or elsewhere during divine service?"[20] When the Bristol society instituted a weekly reformation sermon, he gave the SPCK an account of how it had been done and how much it had pleased the bishop.[21] When the London reformers sent the Bristol society some books, Bedford asked the secretary of the SPCK "to acquaint some of the members of the society for reformation of

17. SPCK, Original Letter No. 87, April 18, 1700.
18. SPCK, Abstract Letter No. 313, June 6, 1701.
19. Ibid., Nos. 218, 346.
20. W. O. B. Allen and Edmund McClure, *Two Hundred Years,* p. 79.
21. SPCK, Abstract Letter No. 226, December 24, 1700.

manners that he has received their parcels." [22] In this way did
the SPCK provide a vital link between the provincial reformers
and the London reforming societies.

In addition the SPCK was a source of strength to the reforming societies through its campaign of dispersing books throughout England. Besides the books on the methods of erecting
charity schools, the SPCK sent out hundreds of copies of the
Account of the Societies for Reformation of Manners, which
one of its correspondents, Mr. Fenwick of Leicestershire,
thought "a book so excellently wrote that I was in great hopes
to have seen a second edition of it before this." [23] The *Help
to a National Reformation* was a book usually included in the
society's packets, and the little handbooks against cursing,
drunkenness, and other vices were sent out in great quantity.[24]
Until the SPCK sent him a copy of the *Account of the Societies
for Reformation of Manners* in 1700, Mr. Ellison of Newcastle
had been totally unfamiliar with the methods used by these
societies in their work.[25] When Mr. Harris of Glamorganshire
wanted to have a local justice furnished with papers relating
to "the business of reformation," he wrote to the SPCK, not to
the reforming societies.[26]

The connection between the SPCK and the reforming societies was of the greatest importance to the cause of a moral
reformation, but it was to be short-lived. The Bristol society
soon became entirely dominated by the SPCK. In effect it was
swallowed up, and giving up prosecutions, it turned to the sup-

22. Ibid., No. 341, September 3, 1701.
23. SPCK, Original Letter No. 94, May 18, 1700. Mr. Fenwick's
hopes were answered. There were new editions of this book in 1700,
1701, 1702, 1704, 1705, and 1706.
24. Wanley MSS, fols. 158–62; SPCK, Abstract Letters No. 1301
(September 5, 1709), and No. 2131 (July 6, 1710).
25. SPCK, Original Letter No. 23, January 27, 1700 (probably
1701).
26. SPCK, Abstract Letter No. 333, August 10, 1701.

port of charity schools. By 1705 its meetings were perfunctory, and after that apparently there were no meetings at all. What happened in Bristol happened elsewhere. Those societies that continued to support informers and prosecute the wicked got little support from the SPCK after 1710. Correspondence with them dwindled steadily. If the reforming societies turned their interest to the education of the poor, they ceased to be, strictly speaking, societies for reformation and became branches of the SPCK. The SPCK continued to distribute publications of the reforming societies, but without the enthusiasm of earlier years. No longer did it buy reformation sermons to send to its correspondents. The London reformers now had to send the sermons to the SPCK and request that they be distributed.[27] Mention of the reforming societies in the correspondence of the SPCK had once been frequent, but after 1710 it was only when these sermons were received that notice was taken of their existence. The SPCK was still interested in the reformation of manners, but not in the societies for reformation.

The SPCK also played a role in aiding the religious societies. Mr. Thomas Frank of Bedfordshire, one of the SPCK's most active correspondents, was especially interested in their work. He hoped that the SPCK would keep a list of all the societies— clerical, religious, and reforming—in England and Wales. Such a list would enable men like him to "know where to enquire for our friends as we have occasion for them." He wrote that it was his wish, and certainly it became the goal of the SPCK, "that all endeavors be used to unite the clergy and laity in this great work of reformation and let their interests and aims be the same." [28] In his letter he urged the society to encourage clergymen who were members of the SPCK to take the reli-

27. Ibid., Nos. 6716, 7704, 12,049, 14,498; and SPCK, Miscellaneous Letters, 4, fol. 86.
28. Wanley MSS, fol. 25.

gious societies of their parishes into their charge. Later, Frank, who had a fondness for harmless conspiracy,[29] set about the formation of a religious society in Dunstable with the help of the SPCK.

> Several young men, having been made acquainted with the religious societies in London, have a desire to form them-selves into a society in Dunstable. Mr. Lord, the vicar, is acquainted with it; he is indeed a pious man but timorous and wants a spur. I'm persuaded if some method could be found out to send a letter to him (from an unknown hand, it matters not) with Mr. Woodward's book of the religious societies, together with Mr. Wesley's letter (which I hope is not printed), it might have some good effect on him. I shall be ready to second it at some convenient distance of time.[30]

The link between the SPCK and the religious societies was more natural and enduring than that with the reforming soci-eties because they were both Anglican. These Anglican socie-ties—and in 1701 there was the addition of the Society for Propagating the Gospel in Foreign Parts—shared the aim of strengthening and spreading the faith of the Church of Eng-land, but—especialy to the two large societies, the SPCK and the SPG—that was not an end in itself. It was a means of im-proving the morality of Englishmen and eventually, it was hoped, of all mankind. These societies, therefore, were in a sense societies for reformation of manners. Their members, like those of the reforming societies, assumed that there had been a great decay of religion and a serious lapse of morality

29. For example see SPCK, Abstract Letter No. 306, May 26, 1701.

30. SPCK, Original Letter No. 91, April 27, 1700. Woodward's book is *An Account of the Rise and Progress of the Religious Soci-eties*, 2d ed. London, 1698. Samuel Wesley wrote many long letters to the SPCK, including some defending the religious societies.

during the reigns of the last Stuart kings. The Anglican societies sought to improve morals primarily through education and through stirring up more enthusiasm for the services of the Church. The reforming societies, consisting as they did of both churchmen and dissenters, attacked vice more directly. But all these societies are a testimony to the intensity of the religious revival after 1689. Perhaps it would be more accurate to call it a moral revival. Even though the Anglican societies relied on the catechism and the Book of Common Prayer, they did not encourage their members to split theological hairs. They preached a broad, ethical religion, a religion for all men, not merely for theologians. Sir Leslie Stephen might have used the publications of any one of these societies to illustrate the process that he considered characteristic of 18th-century thought—the divorce of theology and morality. Reformers would sometimes urge men to be virtuous in order to be saved hereafter, but more often they would urge Englishmen to be virtuous in order to make England strong and safe. These societies were in harmony with a new century that was to be more concerned with morals than with faith.

It was to be not only an age concerned with morals in England, but an age seeking internal peace. During the greater part of the 17th century there had been almost constant strife between Englishmen divided against one another by their differences in religion and politics. The conflicts had been bloody and costly. The apparent rifts in the nation had led James II to hope that he could snuff out those laws and institutions which Englishmen of all persuasions cherished as safeguards of their liberties. After 1689 most men hoped that bloodshed and persecution had ended. Dissenters now enjoyed a degree of toleration, and moderate men of all sects talked more of essential agreement between their various religious beliefs than of the differences.

The idea of reforming manners was one that presumably

could appeal to all. The SPCK and the SPG could not pretend
to comprehend all sects, but their moderate views encouraged
dissenters to come over to the Church without having to strain
their consciences too severely. The societies for reformation
were not so impeded and from the very first made a frank appeal for all sects to join in their work. Edward Stephens made
it clear that the first societies for reformation in London were
formed by Anglicans,[31] but one of these societies sent a description of its work to some dissenting ministers and urged them
to join. They reminded the ministers that "the universal prevalence of profaneness and debauchery" was a subject of sorrow
to men of all sects and begged them to urge members of their
congregations "to follow the example of the persons before
mentioned in making it some part of their business to take
notice of the breaches of the laws and to give informations
against offenders." After some practical instructions about ob-
taining warrants and listing some of the most effective laws
against vice, this paper concluded with the wish that the work
"may prove a very effectual means of promoting kindness and
charity among men of different persuasions as well as provoking and encouraging one another in good works." [32] Here
surely was the spirit of the Toleration Act.

Josiah Woodward and others who wrote in the cause of the
reforming societies made much of the possibilities offered by
them for peace and cooperation between the sects. The societies were open to all men "that have a zeal for God and religion." [33] The danger of vice was apparent to everyone and the

31. Edward Stephens, *The Beginning and Progress of a Needful and Hopeful Reformation* (London, 1691), p. 10.
32. Rawlinson MS D. 129, fols. 6–15.
33. *A Brief Account of the Nature . . . of the Societies for
Reformation of Manners*, pp. 9, 12–13. See also *An Account of the
Societies for Reformation of Manners in London and Westminster*,
pp. 27–8.

work of reformation of equal benefit to all. " 'Tis universal, not confined to sects and parties." [34] Woodward spoke vividly of the good effects of the reformation:

> And since the time that the usefulness of these societies has been visible to the world, their zeal hath provoked some of their dissenting brethren to join with them occasionally and to set up the like among themselves. And who knows but that this essential union of theirs in the love of God and goodness may at last draw them to center in the same communion; and so bring a most inestimable blessing to this bleeding Church and State, than which no blessing upon earth can be imagined greater. For it would mightily strengthen the languishing interest of protestancy and envigorate the power of our holy religion, and be the best and surest foundation of a vigorous and general reformation. [35]

This union of Woodward's was a union within the Church rather than toleration and peace among different sects. The author of *A Short Account of the Several Kinds of Societies,* an Anglican, was more liberal and spoke of the reformation as having brought about a "union of hearts and affections in things so agreeable to all who deserve the name of Protestants, of Christians, of Englishmen, or even Men." [36] In the sermons preached to the reformers, especially in those of dissenting preachers, the same theme is repeated. Edmund Calamy spoke of the "hopeful prognostic in the present case that those who differ in rituals but with too much vehemence should

34. John Dunton, *The Life and Errors of John Dunton,* p. 357.
35. Josiah Woodward, *An Account of the Rise and Progress of the Religious Societies* (3d ed. London, 1701), p. 104.
36. *A Short Account of Several Kinds of Societies* (London? 1700?), p. 2. The author was probably Mr. Justice Hooke, one of the SPCK's founders.

unanimously join together in forming those societies for reformation." [37] In answer to those who censured the societies for
being "blended of several parties," Jabez Earle, a Presbyterian
minister, said, "Sure it's no criminal confederacy when men
join to quench a fire. . . . And as to your consisting of men
that are differently persuaded in the lesser matters of religion,
this is to your honor." [38]

Cooperation was certainly the ideal of the societies. In London the various societies for reformation seemed to work
together and help one another. Usually the Anglicans had
their sermon in one place, the dissenters in another, but a
sermon like Mr. Earle's in 1704 was delivered to a mixed
congregation. In the early days when there were only forty or
fifty reformers in London, most of them were Anglican, but
one or two were dissenters, and they must have met in a society
with the Anglicans.[39] In its constitution the Nottingham society for reformation specifically provided for the admission
of dissenters "provided they be persons of sobriety and integrity." [40] Mr. Gilpin of the diocese of Carlisle, an ardent
reformer and an Anglican, would not consider forming a
society that was not a mixed society.[41]

The evidence here might lead a historian to believe with
the more sanguine reformers that the societies for reformation
of manners in particular and the other societies founded at
this time represented an important step in the direction of
bringing religious peace to England. One would like to believe that these reformers looked upon the extreme religious

37. Edmund Calamy, A Sermon Preach'd before the Societies
for Reformation of Manners (London, 1699), dedication, p. iii,
and p. 43.

38. Jabez Earle, A Sermon Preach'd to the Societies for Reformation of Manners (London, 1704), pp. 35–6.

39. Rawlinson MS D. 129, fol. 8.

40. Thomas Sharp, The Life of John Sharp, 1, 176–7.

41. John Nichols, Letters on Various Subjects . . . to and from
William Nicolson, 1, 185.

controversies of past years as something ridiculous, like the bloodshed in Liliput caused by the emperor's decree that one should break his egg at the small end. The societies might seem to be above the bitter political and religious contests that kept Queen Anne's reign from being a peaceful one at home. But this impression of the benign and pacifying role of the reforming societies is not correct.

One of the most important reasons for the failure of the reforming societies to maintain the popular enthusiasm of their early years was that they were not in fact what they seemed to be. They did not make for internal peace; they were not instruments of toleration. They were centers of controversy from the first and became more and more deeply involved in party and sectarian conflicts. To many Englishmen they appeared not as the heroic army that was to avert a divine judgment but rather as centers of sedition and enemies of the established order in Church and State. This view was not surprising. The very existence of such societies was a criticism of the Church and State, a criticism which the reforming preachers and pamphleteers made explicit. Edward Stephens had lashed out at the corruption of the members of Parliament and the justices of the peace and had warned the king that many of his advisers were wicked men.[42] In a more temperate vein the author of the *Proposals for a National Reformation* criticized the magistrates and the bishops.[43] These statements and the efforts of the societies to oversee the work of magistrates, constables, and churchwardens gave

42. Edward Stephens, *The Beginning and Progress of a Needful and Hopeful Reformation,* "To the King" and pp. 14–15. See also his *Achan and Elymas,* London, 1704; his *The Corruption and Impiety of the Common Members of the Late House of Commons,* London, 1701; and his *To the Knights, Gentlemen, Freeholders, and Commons of England,* London, 1704.
43. *Proposals for a National Reformation of Manners* (London, 1694), pp. 9–14.

weight to the suspicion that the societies were subversive. "Should they long continue," wrote one of their enemies, "and come to maturity and strength, like so many vipers they'd eat out the bowels of the Established Church, their mother. But what did I say, the Church their mother? That I recant. They are only seedlings of the good old cause and sprouts of the Rebellion of '41." [44]

The letters and proclamations of William and Mary had led the reformers and others to believe that their work had the support of the government. But secretly the king and his advisers were suspicious of the activities of men acting in the cause of reformation, particularly because of the dissenters involved in the work. In June 1698 William Taylor, a dissenting minister of Newbury, wrote a letter to Mr. Saunders, another dissenting minister of Oxford. The letter by mistake was delivered to another Mr. Saunders who was the chaplain of All Souls College. The Anglican Mr. Saunders turned the letter over to William Nicolson, the archdeacon of Carlisle. The letter began:

> I had a letter last week by the direction of the committee of ministers and gentlemen appointed at London for settling a correspondence of the protestant dissenting ministers and congregations throughout this kingdom for the advancement of the interest of religion and reformation of manners with the articles there agreed upon in order thereunto and a desire to communicate them speedily to the brethren in these parts, that, if possible, a general meeting may be had this summer in London. [45]

Mr. Taylor then invited Saunders to attend the meeting in London and informed him of a plan to have a general meeting

44. [Philalethes] *Plain Dealing in Answer to Plain English,* p. 17.
45. John Nichols, ed., *Letters on Various Subjects . . . to and from William Nicolson, 1,* 109.

of dissenting ministers and congregations in Newbury on
June 22 to consider the proposals for reformation made by
the London committee. Probably through Nicolson the
dissenters' plans became known to officials in London: to
Lord Chancellor Somers and to James Vernon, the principal
secretary of state. In two letters written in July 1698 Vernon
communicated to the Duke of Shrewsbury the fears felt by
those in power concerning the growing numbers of societies
formed "under the pretense of a reformation of manners."
Vernon told Shrewsbury that Archbishop Sharp thought
"their design may be to undermine the Church, and my Lord
Chancellor thinks they rather aim at discrediting the administration which they represent as atheistical and designing
to drive Christianity out of the world." The king was anxious
that the meetings be observed, and Vernon suggested to
Shrewsbury that a Mr. Griffith, an independent minister over
whom Shrewsbury had some influence, be used as a spy re-
porting either to Vernon or Somers. "He need not be shy of
opening himself as to the innocent part of it, which may concern their own congregations only; for that, giving no jealousy
to the government, will not be made use of to create them
any disturbance; but the thing we would know is what discontented churchmen or discarded statesmen mean by in-
sinuating themselves into their familiarities." "There will be
some other ways likewise taken to come at the bottom of this
machination." One other way that Vernon found was to question tactfully one Mr. Owen, a Presbyterian minister who was,
as Vernon phrased it, "considerable among the dissenters."
From him he learned what he could have learned from reading Edward Stephens' *Beginning and Progress.* Among other
things, he learned of the reformers' efforts to curtail swearing
through the use of anonymous informers. Mr. Owen admitted that the procedure was not "according to the received
rules of law that provides no man shall be condemned un-

heard and that the party may expect to have his accuser face
to face, but he thinks it justifiable by the prerogative of the
King of Heaven, whose honor ought to be vindicated by extraordinary methods." It was Vernon's opinion that "such an
inquisition will not be borne in this kingdom, let the pretense
be what it will."

> I find these reformers are people of all persuasions, as
> well churchmen as dissenters, so that it is not the interest
> of any particular sect they would promote, but the general
> good of mankind by introducing a conformity of manners
> and a primitive purity. This is a pretty temper to be worked
> upon if designing persons get amongst them, and if they
> grow to any strength. I know not what models they have
> for establishing saintship. I am inclined to be of opinion
> that this may be a way to set up hypocrisy, but will not
> much advance real honesty or virtue, and when men have
> run through the circle of severities that are almost in-
> separable from a sudden reformation, they will return to
> a natural state of being as good or as bad as they please.[46]

How wise of Mr. Secretary Vernon! The accuracy of his information about the societies was subject to question, but he
saw that some of the societies' practices were intolerable, and
he predicted correctly the outcome of their work.

Some men of high position in the Church were even more
disturbed than Vernon by the existence of the societies for
reformation. Generally speaking, Low churchmen approved
and encouraged them, while those with High leanings looked
upon them with varying degrees of distrust. Whiggish bishops
like Wake of Lincoln, Lloyd of Worcester, Fowler of Gloucester, and Stratford of Chester spoke and wrote in their praise.

46. These letters are dated July 16 and 21, 1698, and are printed
in G. P. R. James, ed., *Letters Illustrative of the Reign of William
III* (London, 1841), 2, 128–30, 133–4. Griffith's report on the Newbury meeting is printed ibid., 2, 156–7.

Lloyd and Stratford distributed the societies' literature on their visitations.[47] Archbishop Tenison, seeing no danger in them, tolerated them within the province of Canterbury. But Archbishop Sharp of York was a different sort of man. He could not be called a "high-flyer"; he was a moderate High churchman and Tory. His attitude toward the societies was not so friendly as Tenison's.

The first reforming society to come to Sharp's attention was one at Nottingham. Early in 1698 this society wrote him for permission to institute a quarterly sermon. Taken by surprise, Sharp approved with some reservations. He was disturbed because the society already was a flourishing affair, and he asked to have a copy of its rules and orders. Comparing their rules with what he took to be the rules of the London societies for reformation—actually the rules of the religious societies —he immediately noted that the London society was open only to communicants of the Church of England, while the Nottingham society was open to all persons of sobriety and integrity. Although he asserted that he was not opposed to a society that comprehended all sects, he forbad the Anglican clergymen of Nottingham to give the quarterly sermons to such a society.[48] His position was a cautious one and in many ways confused. He was not sure that the societies were legal. He was quite certain that it was contrary to the canons of the Church of England for a minister to join such a society.[49] Although his opposition to these societies became generally known, the Nottingham society continued, and another was founded at

47. William Wake, *Charge to the Clergy of His Diocese in His Primary Visitation Begun at Lincoln, May 20, 1706* (London, 1707), p. 33; Wake, *A Sermon Preach'd to the Societies for Reformation of Manners* (London, 1706); David L. Robertson, ed., *Diary of Francis Evans, Secretary to Bishop Lloyd, 1699–1706* (Oxford, 1903), p. 15; John Nichols, *Letters on Various Subjects . . . to and from William Nicolson, 1*, 170–2, 177.

48. Thomas Sharp, *The Life of John Sharp, 1*, 170–80.

49. The canons that applied to this matter were the 12th and 73d.

Hull. He succeeded for some time in squelching moves to form a society in York.

It was the societies in the diocese of Carlisle that caused him the greatest concern. William Nicolson, then the Archdeacon of Carlisle, aroused Sharp to the danger in that diocese. Nicolson's violent opposition to the societies seems to have been assumed for the purpose of currying favor with the Archbishop; for in 1706, after he had been made Bishop of Carlisle, Nicolson delivered a sermon to the London societies. Nicolson called Sharp's attention to the reforming societies in the diocese of Carlisle in February 1699/1700, when the chancellor of the diocese, Thomas Tullie, joined with eight other men, "one whereof is the most violent Independent in the diocese and others notoriously disaffected to our ecclesiastical discipline," to form a society for reformation at Carlisle.[50] The situation there was complicated because Thomas Smith, the Bishop of Carlisle, was eighty-five years old and sick, incapable, in Nicolson's opinion, of acting to suppress this society "with that briskness which the case requires."[51] Bishop Smith had been gulled by Thomas Bray, one of the founders of the SPCK, into adding his name to a list of bishops who were supposed to have approved of the societies for reformation.[52] The chancellor had believed that his bishop approved when he saw his name among the others, and some clergymen at Brampton had joined a society there, having been encouraged by the example of the bishop and the chancellor. Nicolson and Sharp agreed that matters were getting out of hand. The bishop was perplexed, the chancellor stubborn. Finally, prodded by Nicol-

50. John Nichols, *Letters on Various Subjects . . . to and from William Nicolson, 1,* 146–7.

51. Ibid., p. 152.

52. Ibid., pp. 145–7. The list of approving bishops was published in the *Account of the Societies for Reformation of Manners in London and Westminster.*

son, who came armed with a letter from Sharp, the bishop rebuked the chancellor and issued instructions to his clergy to
do everything in their power to encourage a reformation, but
to join a society only if it were made up of staunch churchmen.[53] Nicolson was certain that this would force Tullie to
give up his connection with the dissenters, but the society in
Carlisle survived, only one or two dropping out when they
learned the true attitude of the bishop. Nicolson was delighted,
however, that Tullie, "the little man" as he called him, lost
much of his influence with the clergy as a result of his actions.[54]

The attitudes of Sharp and Nicolson were typical of the
objections of other moderately High churchmen. They approved of the idea of a reformation of manners; they might
even approve of the societies for that purpose. Sharp said
reluctantly that he would approve of the Carlisle society or
a society at York if they would pay more attention to prayer,
the taking of communion, and "to the diligent attendance upon
catechizing and instruction the youth of their parishes in the
principles of Christianity, the practice of which things will in
my poor opinion more contribute to the promoting a reformation than the informing against criminals, though that is a
good work too"; [55] in other words Sharp would approve of
these societies if they were religious societies. The real stumbling block for these men was the cooperation with dissenters.

Nicolson was not so mild in his opinions as Sharp. Having
read an account of the societies in Bedfordshire and Buckinghamshire, he wrote, "I am very much troubled at the perusal
of it as foreseeing the ruin which such societies (if not
discountenanced) must speedily bring on the Established

53. Thomas Sharp, *The Life of John Sharp*, *1*, 185–7; John Nichols, *Letters on Various Subjects . . . to and from William Nicolson*,
1, 145, 152–3, 161, 163–4.
54. Nichols, *1*, 150–1, 154.
55. Thomas Sharp, *The Life of John Sharp*, *1*, 188.

Church." [56] He thought the societies were anabaptistical, too much like "leagues and covenants" of past times that had led to bloodshed. "Separate societies and councils of reformation have always been reckoned necessary implements towards the subverting of an Establishment, and so we find them insisted on in the 'Jesuits' Memorial', &c." The societies were institutions dangerous to Church and State.[57] Because of men with opinions like these, pious reformers found their work hindered by official disapproval and distrust.[58]

Higher churchmen than Sharp and Nicolson held any manner of association suspect. Even the clerical societies, recommended by Archbishop Tenison and the SPCK, were discouraged by some prelates. The Bishop of Exeter was an enemy of every kind of society.[59] Ministers who received the circular letter of the SPCK showed their fear of organizations of this sort in their cautious replies, saying that they must try to get the approval of their bishops before entering into such a combination.[60] Archbishop Sharp, although essentially averse to any "confederacy or combinations, whether of clergy or otherwise," with some misgivings approved of the formation of clerical societies in his province.[61]

The societies for reformation were taken by surprise. The members were so thoroughly convinced of the righteousness of their cause and the benefits of their work to the nation that the

56. John Nichols, *Letters on Various Subjects . . . to and from William Nicolson, 1,* 153.

57. Ibid., *1,* 147–8, 153–4.

58. For example see W. O. B. Allen and Edmund McClure, *Two Hundred Years,* pp. 68, 79, 81–2; and SPCK, Original Letter No. 23, January 27, 1699/1700.

59. SPCK, Abstract Letter No. 125, June 30, 1700.

60. SPCK, Abstract Letter No. 32, February 15, 1699/1700; SPCK, Original Letters Nos. 19, January 20, 1699/1700; 29, February 12, 1699/1700; 60, March 4, 1699/1700.

61. Thomas Sharp, *The Life of John Sharp, 1,* 182, 184–5. SPCK, Original Letter No. 20, February 14, 1699/1700.

need to assure others that their work in no way interfered with Church or State did not at first occur to them. It soon became clear that such assurance was necessary. A group of men in London formed a society for reformation in June 1693 and at a later time saw fit to add to their original paper of agreement the words, "and that in our said meeting we never meddle with affairs of Church or State." [62] The ministers who gave sermons to the societies usually attempted to answer the objections. "There is no evil (whatever any may mistakenly surmise or maliciously suggest) designed by them against either Church or State," said Mr. Billingsley.[63] Mr. Palmer in his sermon took note of the criticisms: " 'Tis said then that to form such societies to enquire into other men's faults and execute penal statutes upon 'em, is combination, maintenance, and champerty, forbidden by the law and too officious and busy a work for a wise and good man to engage in." [64] He answered with the assertion that the crimes that the societies fought were so prevalent and influential that "extraordinary methods ought to be used to conquer them." [65] John Galpine assured the societies that from the earliest times Satan and his forces had tried to represent Christianity as something dangerous to the authority of the State.[66]

Edward Stephens had never tried to answer this sort of argument; indeed, his violent manner gave cause for such

62. Rawlinson MS D. 129, fol. 2. This phrase was inserted above the line in a different hand.

63. John Billingsley, *A Sermon Preach'd to the Societies for Reformation of Manners* (London, 1706), p. 7.

64. Samuel Palmer, *A Sermon Preach'd to the Societies for Reformation of Manners* (London, 1706), p. 27. Maintenance and champerty are terms in law referring to illegal meddling with a cause pending.

65. Ibid., p. 29.

66. John Galpine, *A Sermon Preach'd . . . before the Societies for Reformation* (London, 1703), p. 13.

fears. Josiah Woodward, writing a few years later, was well aware of these criticisms, and much of his work was directed at those who feared the reforming societies as dangerous and meddlesome innovations. He tried to make the reforming societies as nearly equivalent to the religious societies as he could in order to make it seem that they were not something new or something that strict Anglicans should fear. He succeeded in confusing some of his contemporaries—and some later historians—but Archbishop Sharp for one, after some initial doubts, saw through Woodward's argument and quickly distinguished between the societies for reformation and other groups. "But as for the societies for reformation that are now on foot in several places, they are new things . . . for which there is no foundation in our laws and canons." [67]

As the societies for reformation spread through England, the conflicts surrounding them also spread. All the assurances of Woodward and others like him did little to win for the societies the universal approval that they anticipated. The doubts and objections still existed; the societies for reformation, and even the SPCK and its clerical societies, became political issues. According to John Dunton, a reformer was presumed to be a Whig—a "sneaking, pitiful Whig." [68] The author of one of the attacks on William Bisset's *Plain English* said that Bisset "has plainly showed us which way the societies for reformation of manners drive; we may evidently see Whiggism entirely taints the members thereof; and, if they embrace Mr. Bisset's tenets, are ready to imbibe the principles of faction and rebellion." [69] It was natural that members of the societies should be Whiggish; few Tories would care to join with dissenters in any effort of this kind. Few High churchmen would admit that the services of the Church were inadequate to reform manners. Their

67. Thomas Sharp, *The Life of John Sharp,* 1, 184–5.
68. John Dunton, *The Night-Walker,* No. 2, pp. 2, 17.
69. Isaac Sharpe, *Plain English Made Plainer,* preface.

care for strict discipline in the Church would make them distrust any independent societies of a religious nature.[70]

By 1702 the whole question of a reformation of manners was involved in heated party conflicts. In that year Bishop Lloyd of Worcester and his son were accused by Sir John Pakington of having tried to influence the voters against him in the parliamentary election of that year. Pakington maintained that Lloyd had used his high position to slander Pakington, spreading the story that he was a Jacobite, a drunkard and whoremaster, and a man opposed to any reformation of manners. Lloyd was supposed to have sent into his diocese a pamphlet bitterly denouncing Pakington, which Lloyd called simply a pamphlet "for promoting the most pious designs of reformation." [71] Pakington made an excellent case against the bishop, and the House of Commons petitioned the queen to remove Lloyd from his position as lord almoner, which she did.

The incident did not end there. It served to bring from his relative obscurity the Reverend Henry Sacheverell, who came to Pakington's defense with *The Character of a Low-Churchman,* a virulent attack on all those men who, in Sacheverell's opinion, had emasculated the Church. In the course of this tirade he singled out Bishop Lloyd and his defense of the work of reformation of manners. Sacheverell's Low churchman "is always declaiming against the vice of the age and the insufficiency of our laws to restrain it; and more securely to cloak it, he screens himself under a pretended society to reform it." "This specious pretense to godliness and sanctified railing against vice smells so strong of the pharisee that 'tis

70. Not all High churchmen disapproved of the societies. Robert Nelson, for example, supported them. See C. F. Secretan, *Memoirs of the Life and Times of the Pious Robert Nelson,* p. 96. For others who saw in them an indirect means of increasing the civil power of the clergy, see below, pp. 97–9.

71. *The Evidence Given at the Bar of the House of Commons upon the Complaint of Sir John Pakington against William, Lord Bishop of Worcester* (London, 1702), pp. 11–12.

always to be suspected to be the mask and disguise of hypocrisy." [72] He hated Lloyd and men like him because now they cried out for reformation and for more discipline while they were the ones who had done most to make the Church powerless. Such was the beginning of Sacheverell's career as a Tory pamphleteer and the beginning of his war with the reformers. On August 15, 1709, Sacheverell delivered the assize sermon at Derby in which he railed violently against the societies for reformation. His text was from St. Paul, "Lay hands suddenly on no man, neither be partaker of other men's sins." [73] From this text he spoke on one's duty toward sinners, making it clear that only those with some official authority should concern themselves with the crimes of others. In private conversation, although one should advise, warn, and rebuke a sinner,

> charity, religion, and justice oblige us with equal force and penalty to the no less necessary duties of peace and quietness, forbearance and forgiveness, in mercy, compassion, and good nature to cover and conceal our brother's sins and infirmities. Do not these as strictly command us not to thrust ourselves pragmatically into his business, or meddle with those concerns that do not belong to us, or under the sanctified pretense of reformation of manners to turn informer, assume an odious and factious office, arrogantly intrench upon other's Christian liberty and innocence, and under the show of more zeal and purity (the most infallible token of a dextrous and refined hypocrite and knave) turn the world upside down, and set all mankind into quarrels and confusions? . . . But . . . we must strictly observe that these duties are always confined to overt acts and visible cases; for religion has left in this matter wide room for the right exercise of our prudence and discretion; for

72. *The Character of a Low–Churchman* (London? 1702), pp. 14, 18.
73. I Timothy 5:22.

it does not oblige us to charge men at random upon bare
surmise and suspicion, or to pry officiously into their lives
and secret affairs, and to invade their private rights by
usurping a jurisdiction which we have no title to justify,
or with a rude air of superiority to obtrude ourselves upon
'em as privy-counsellors and dogmatically censure, rebuke,
or advise in our neighbor's proceedings that don't belong
to us, neither lie under the verge of our cognizance. Whatever godly and fallacious glosses such troublesome wasps
that erect themselves into illegal inquisitors may cast upon
their actions, they are doubtless the unwarrantable effects
of an idle, encroaching, impertinent, and meddling curi-
osity. . . . It is in short the base product of ill-nature,
spiritual pride, censoriousness, and sanctified spleen, pre-
tending to carry on the blessed work of reformation by
lying, slandering, whispering, backbiting, and tale-bearing,
the most express character of the devil, who is emphatically
styled the grand accuser of the brethren.[74]

This telling attack came at a time when the societies had
been active long enough to have provoked numbers of Englishmen. Their work was well known; rumors of their arbitrary
treatment of suspected offenders were commonplace. This
sermon came to be famous after the delivery of Sacheverell's
even more famous sermon, *The Perils of False Brethren,* in St.
Paul's a few months later. According to John Dunton, Sacheverell repeated his indictment of the reformers in his St.
Paul's sermon, but that section was omitted from the published
version.[75] There is no evidence to support his assertion, but
in any event Sacheverell's attitude toward reformation of manners was one of the issues of the impeachment proceedings

74. Henry Sacheverell, *The Communication of Sin* (London,
1709), pp. 14–15, 20–1.
75. John Dunton, *The Bull-Baiting, or Sach—ll Dress'd up in
Fireworks* (London, 1709), "Epistle Dedicatory" and pp. 13–15.

brought against him by the Whig administration and based on the dedication of his Derby sermon and on the entire text of his sermon at St. Paul's. In addition to the formal charges brought against him, he was, in the course of the trial, accused of being an enemy of reformation. Reformers like Dunton and William Bisset did much to make Sacheverell the symbol of all the forces opposed to reformation, just as the Whig politicians tried to make him the symbol of Tory treachery.[76] When Sacheverell was convicted, the reformers might have considered their societies and methods vindicated, had it not been that his conviction proved disastrous to the faction which had impeached him. Sacheverell became a popular hero—a remarkable fact when one considers that he walked in triumph in the wake of the seven bishops, the advocate of passive obedience almost in the train of those men who defied the king. That a great shift in popular opinion had occurred in twenty years was obvious from the cheering which greeted Sacheverell and from the victory of the Tories at the election after his trial. It did not seem to be the desire for peace which accounted for the Tories' popularity: they did not make an issue of the war until after the election.[77] Sacheverell was the issue. His popularity can in part be explained by his ability to act the role of defender of popular rights and liberties. He could accuse the Whigs, because of their supposed connection with the societies for reformation, of failing to respect an Englishman's rights before the law, of condoning the conviction of a man who had not seen his accuser face to face, of approving the use of irregular warrants. Therefore the societies were in part re-

76. Ibid., passim. William Bisset, *The Modern Fanatick*, and his *Fair Warning* (London, 1710), passim. For an account of the trial and the way in which the reformation of manners entered into it, see *The Tryal of Dr. Henry Sacheverell* (London, 1710), pp. 114, 206, 229, 236–7.

77. Mary Ransome, "The Press in the General Election of 1710," *Cambridge Historical Journal, 6* (1939), 209–21.

sponsible for the Whigs' downfall, and Sacheverell himself, through his denunciations of their methods, did much to damage the societies. After 1710 one could easily forget their existence. Their activities were inconspicuous: never again did they arouse the enthusiasm of 1691 or 1700. Sacheverell's accusations dogged them.[78] Even in 1715 one minister made his reformation sermon a reply to the Derby sermon of six years before.[79] The Sacheverell affair made it clear that a reformation of manners was not something universally agreed upon, something apart from sordid political squabbles.

Before this time, and in a much quieter way, the interest in the reformation of manners had been used by some ambitious clergymen in the hope of increasing their civil power. Vernon had suspected that the societies for reformation might be ideal instruments for discontented men to use against the government. Nicolson could not imagine why churchmen would enter a society for reformation "unless it be that they think of raising their own fortunes by these uncommon methods, after the more ordinary means of gratifying their ambition have failed them." [80] No one knew how far the revolution might go. The years after 1689 were years of change, a time when ambitious men could hope to gain power with greater ease than they could if institutions had been more stable. Some clergymen saw in the new enthusiasm for a reformation of manners an opportunity to return to the days "when the sword of the ecclesiastical ruler was a terror to evildoers, and the amputations of it more dreadful than of the temporal." [81] Country clergymen, in particular—clergymen interested in the cause

78. Matthew Clarke, *A Sermon Preach'd to the Societies for Reformation of Manners,* pp. 18–19.

79. Samuel Wright, *A Sermon Preached before the Societies for Reformation of Manners.*

80. John Nichols, *Letters on Various Subjects . . . to and from William Nicolson,* 1, 154.

81. Thomas Bisse, *The Ordinance and Office of the Magistrate* (London, 1726), p. 32.

of reformation like James Smith of Cambridgeshire or Samuel Wesley of Lincolnshire—felt that reforming societies, although they might serve the cause in cities, were difficult to organize in the country and relatively ineffective.[82] William Wills of Dowlish Wake near Ilminster, Somerset, wrote to Archbishop Tenison after having received the archbishop's circular letter of April 1699. Wills was especially exercised about the danger of "alehouses, alias hell-houses" which to him were "devil's schools and nurseries of profaneness." In order to combat their influence he suggested to the archbishop that the clergy be made capable of taking affidavits, since in the countryside the justices were often so distant that a reformer could not easily swear out a statement against an offender. From the conspiratorial Thomas Frank of Bedfordshire the archbishop received a paper entitled "Reasons to Induce the Queen's Majesty to Intrust Some of the Clergy in the Several Parts of This Kingdom with Commissions for the Peace." In it he wrote:

> The present endeavors of reformation by suppressing profaneness and vice loudly demand the assistance of the clergy in this juncture. Time indeed was then the Church had a discipline and could put a stop to open immoralities, but we have here publicly lamented the want of that for above 150 years, and therefore the Church, being confined to persuasives and exhortations, hath lost its authority, and vice is grown impudent and daring. So that if the power of the civil magistrate be not strenuously exerted, the nation must be overrun with a torrent of impiety.[83]

His solution was, of course, to make clergymen members of the commission of the peace in their counties, a solution that appealed also to the SPCK. Archdeacon Booth of Durham was

82. SPCK, Original Letter No. 61, March 8, 1699/1700; and W. O. B. Allen and McClure, *Two Hundred Years*, p. 88.

83. Lambeth MS 933, fol. 34. Ibid., 942, fol. 152. SPCK, Abstract Letter No. 288, April 28, 1701.

an active reformer and a justice of the peace as well. His double capacity delighted the SPCK, whose secretary expressed the hope that the example of his good work "will soon take away the present prejudice that our clergy should not be entrusted with any civil power, but keep only to their church and profession." [84]

The hopes of these men were to be fulfilled. Since the 16th century there had always been a few bishops and clergymen who were at the same time magistrates. In the 18th century such men became common, and they proved their worth. They had a better knowledge of the law than the laymen; they were more careful and diligent in their duties than most other magistrates. Later in the century, when societies for reformation were again formed, these clerical magistrates took the lead in organizing them and furthering their work. [85]

The hopes the reformers had that the societies would do their work in peace and harmony were dashed. Josiah Woodward's efforts to make them seem proper to High churchmen and tolerant to Low churchmen and dissenters were doomed to failure. By trying to have it both ways he created conflict rather than harmony. The High churchmen were not to be pacified so easily, and the blending of Church and Dissent was not successful. The Carlisle society may have included men of all sects, but in Derby there were two societies, one of churchmen and one of dissenters, which competed with each other more than they cooperated. [86] The attempt to include all sects within the societies was a source of weakness, not of strength. One of the advantages of the SPCK was its strictly Anglican complexion. [87]

84. Wanley MSS, fol. 48.
85. Sidney and Beatrice Webb, *English Local Government. The Parish and the County* (London, 1924), pp. 350–60.
86. SPCK, Abstract Letter No. 288, April 28, 1701.
87. For example see SPCK, Original Letter No. 14, January 8, 1699/1700.

While the societies for reformation failed to commend themselves to Englishmen as instruments of peace and toleration, they might have succeeded in appealing to the developing charitable impulses of the nation; for charity was more of a concern to Englishmen in the 18th century than it had been before. They seemed to become more humane and more aware of the existence of cruelty in everyday life. The popular appeal of the charity schools might have been shared by their fellow instruments of reformation, the societies, which were equally charitable. "Reformation is a branch of charity, and . . . you must act in it, as with courage, so with great candor and tenderness, with a heart melting with pity." [88] It was charity to rebuke the wicked; it was an act of kindness to a hardened sinner to have him punished.[89] It was clearly the charitable duty of every Christian to be a reformer; for Christ himself was the "best reformer," and "we ourselves promised, when we entered into the Christian covenant in baptism, whereby we were made members of a society instituted by Christ for the reformation of manners," to reform in His way, the way of charity.[90] Richard Willis told the societies that their work was not only "the greatest charity" toward men's souls, but charity as well to the country, in that reformation tended to prevent disorders.[91] But the talk of the humane and charitable nature of the societies' work sounded hollow. The SPCK was a far more convincing venture in charity and practical religion. The men who gave

88. John Heylyn, *A Sermon Preached to the Societies for Reformation of Manners* (London, 1721), p. 23.

89. Robert Drew, *A Sermon Preached to the Societies for Reformation of Manners*, p. 10.

90. Samuel Smith, *A Sermon Preached to the Societies for Reformation of Manners*, p. 14. See also John Leng, *A Sermon Preached to the Societies for Reformation of Manners* (London, 1719), p. 7; and Edmund Gibson, *A Sermon Preached to the Societies for Reformation of Manners* (2d ed. London, 1723), p. 11.

91. *A Sermon Preached . . . to the Societies for Reformation of Manners*, pp. 31–2.

sermons to the reforming societies might speak in terms of practical, rational, natural religion, but their sermons still seemed to many to be superstitious and fanatical, reminiscent of the oppressive enthusiasm of the puritans in the mid-17th century. The morality for which the societies strove was not the popular morality of the 18th century. The moral ideals of the societies were not the neoclassical ideals of wisdom and virtue. The societies worked for virtue without wisdom, the negative virtues of not swearing, not whoring, not profaning the Lord's day. The difference between good and bad was simple and obvious. The good life required no thought.[92] The charity of the reforming societies was a harsh charity; to force a man to be saved was hardly considered to be a charity at all. Far more popular objects of generosity were the charity schools, which were designed to serve the same purpose of reformation.

But a man interested in the reformation of manners for charitable reasons or any other reasons did not necessarily have to turn to the reforming societies or to any of the other societies for promoting Christian behavior. He could support other projects for reformation. This was, as Swift called it, a "projecting age."[93] The word "project" was used at this time to mean some scheme, usually of an ingenious but simple nature, which would have a remarkable effect in bettering the lot of man. The undertaking of the societies for reformation was a typical project in this sense. By the comparatively simple means of encouraging men to inform against moral offenders, England would be converted in a short time into a virtuous nation. There were projects put forward at this time for the improve-

92. For example see Samuel Chandler, *The Necessary and Immutable Difference between Moral Good and Evil* (London, 1738), and William Wishart, "The Certain and Unchangeable Difference betwixt Moral Good and Evil," *Discourses on Several Subjects* (London, 1753), pp. 177–226.
93. Swift, "A Project for the Advancement of Religion," *Works*, 3, 28.

ment of almost everything. The Royal Society had a project in hand for the improvement of English prose style. Men like Sprat and Wilkins believed that if writers would give up the involved eloquence and tricks of rhetoric so popular with most authors in the 17th century, all that was true and good would soon be revealed so clearly that mankind could not fail to see the right path to a golden future. Evil and error had flourished in the wilderness of an involved syntax; in clear, short sentences only truth could exist.[94] The reformation of style was a project to make truth triumphant; the reformation of manners was a project to make virtue triumphant. Aside from the societies and charity schools there were a great number of projects for moral improvement. Swift and Defoe offered solutions to the problem of wickedness that did not make use of societies and informers. *The Tatler* and *The Spectator* were in themselves projects for reformation. Addison and Steele hoped through them to offer examples of virtue that Englishmen would do well to imitate, and at the same time they intended to expose the folly of certain persons whom they had seen acting in an unmannerly way in public.[95] London enjoyed this method of reform. Addison and Steele entertained while they were at their reforming work. Their references to wayward noblemen were always jocular and amusing; without sneering themselves, they hoped to teach the rest to sneer. Their successful journals were not the first of their kind in the way of reforming projects. Ned Ward, in 1698, had started a periodical called *The London Spy; the Vanities and Vices of*

94. See Richard F. Jones, "Science and English Prose Style in the Third Quarter of the Seventeenth Century," *PMLA, 45* (1930), 977–1009.

95. See *The Tatler* No. 3 (April 16, 1709), No. 30 (June 18, 1709), No. 39 (July 7, 1709), No. 89 (November 3, 1709); and *The Spectator*, No. 58 (May 7, 1711). For the way in which persons mentioned in these papers were identified, see Hist. MSS. Comm., *Portland MSS, 4,* 522–3; and James J. Cartwright, ed., *The Wentworth Papers, 1705–1739* (London, 1883), pp. 93, 97.

the Town Exposed to View, and he was the author of several other works describing the vices of the age. The bookseller, John Dunton, was the author of one of the most remarkable reforming periodicals, *The Night-Walker, or Evening Rambles in Search after Lewd Women with the Conferences Held with Them, &c, to Be Published Monthly 'till a Discovery Be Made of All the Chief Prostitutes in England from the Pensionary Miss Down to the Common Strumpet.*[96]

These literary projects enjoyed a great vogue. Indeed, during the period after 1689, the great number of outlandish projects offered to the public made the very name ludicrous. In *Gulliver's Travels* Swift uses the word in a scornful way, and Defoe called the name "projector" a "despicable title." [97] The humorless project of the societies and their long-faced members made them fit subjects for jokes, not only of rakes but of other reformers. *The Spectator* was quite seriously a reforming journal, but its authors wanted to reform England gently, with a smile rather than with a warrant.

Scorned as projects, hated for their use of informers, distrusted as evil and dangerous combinations and as sources of "new and false opinions," [98] the societies for reformation were doomed to failure as instruments of reform. It is safe to say that Addison, Steele, Defoe, Swift, and Jeremy Collier—none of them working through the societies—did far more to reform English morals and manners than the societies with all their informers, pamphlets, sermons, and warrants. The SPCK with its kinder and slower methods was far more effective in its work of reforming, and with its superior form of organization it has survived to the present time. But the societies for reformation cannot be considered a complete failure. They had

96. This was published from March 1695/6 to March 1696/7. It is now very rare, the only copy I have found being in the Library of Congress.

97. Defoe, *An Essay upon Projects,* p. ii.

98. SPCK, Original Letter No. 91, April 29, 1700.

preached moral reform, and though their own methods were discredited, they aroused others to seek different paths to a reformation. Of more lasting importance was their preaching on the necessity of voluntary associations to accomplish a great reformation.

A man working alone could do little directly to stem the activities of wicked men. A few zealots had tried with little success to reform manners by their individual efforts. One man had gone around London and other parts of the country forcing coffee houses to close their doors on Sunday "till it grew too hot for him, till the gentlemen threatened to have his brains beat out and a justice of the peace to lay him by the heels." [99] The mayor of Deal, Thomas Powell, took upon his shoulders the task of reforming the town single-handed. As soon as he was sworn in as mayor in August 1703, he started a campaign against the wicked by giving orders and going around himself to see that they were obeyed. On his first Sunday in office he put a seaman in the stocks for profane swearing; he caught a prostitute, brought her to the whipping post, and had her given twenty lashes; he heard that "five and twenty such like characters left the town, taking the road to Canterbury and Chatham, uttering the most fearful oaths and vowing vengeance on me for what I was doing." At church that day the congregation had sung part of the seventy-fifth Psalm, "and at particular verses which were very appropriate to certain persons present, I stood up, spreading my hands, pointing round the church to some whose ill lives I knew as well as their conversations, which this psalm most peculiarly hinted at." "Some people said I was mad." His colleagues soon complained of his actions, and the people started to ignore his orders. His work brought him little happiness and Deal little reformation; his friends

99. SPCK, Abstract Letter No. 368, December 20, 1701, in Harley MS 7190, fol. 15.

slighted him, and he was lampooned cruelly in song and verse.[100]

Because of the failure of men like Thomas Powell, the advocates of reform put a great emphasis on the forming of societies. Josiah Woodward made it one of his chief subjects.[101] The reformers realized that a society could have a life of its own, survive its founders and have an influence greater than the influence of its individual members.[102] Wicked men and papists knew this to be true; they formed convivial clubs and the Society of Jesus. "As soon as churchmen (so-called) and dissenters shall be but as wise as Roman serpents" and, like them, form societies, protestantism and virtue would thrive.[103] These arguments had considerable effect. Before 1660 and even before 1689 it never could have been said that "we are of all nations the most forward to run into clubs, parties, and societies." [104] But after 1689 clubs and societies mushroomed everywhere, a phenomenon that travelers noticed as something peculiar to the English nation.[105] The island seemed to be swept by a fever that led men to join groups. To pious men the sight was not a happy one. Most of the new organizations seemed to be engines of the devil "for promoting infidelity,

100. This account of Thomas Powell is taken from the parts of his diary published in Stephen Pritchard, *A History of Deal* (Deal, 1864), pp. 156–63.

101. Josiah Woodward, *An Account of the Rise and Progress of the Religious Societies* (3d ed. London, 1701), p. 12.

102. *An Account of the Progress of the Reformation of Manners* (12th ed. London, 1704), pp. 20–2. See also the sermons to the societies for reformation by John Billingsley (London, 1706), p. 10; Moses Lowman (London, 1720), pp. 21–2; Francis Hare (London, 1731), pp. 22–3; and William Simpson (London, 1738), p. 15.

103. Daniel Burgess, *The Golden Snuffers* (London, 1697), p. vi.

104. David Fordyce, *Dialogues Concerning Education* (London, 1745), pp. 61–2.

105. John Macky, *A Journey through England* (2d ed. London, 1722), 1, 286–7. First published in 1712.

the ridicule of scriptures, and blasphemy itself." [106] Therefore good men decided to fight fire with fire. They borrowed the idea of association from the papists, from the wicked, and from business enterprises; they looked upon their societies as righteous societies of Jesus, pious clubs, moral joint-stock companies. [107] As associations the reforming societies had many flaws, but the SPCK and other groups learned from their failure. If the societies for reformation had had the central organization of the SPCK and with it the diligent secretaries —men like John Chamberlain and Humphrey Wanley—to keep all the local groups in hand, they might have survived. From their failure others saw more clearly the way to success.

It has been said recently by an English scholar that

> the habit of forming voluntary associations for every sort of social purpose is widely spread and deeply rooted in this country. Quite naturally in Britain when a man has a new enthusiasm he buys a twopenny notebook, prints 'Minute Book' carefully on the first page, calls together some of his friends under the name of a committee—and behold a new voluntary society is launched. [108]

This is certainly true; the numbers of brass plaques on Bloomsbury doorways are sufficient evidence. Englishmen have looked upon these societies with pride, for they seem to be visible signs of English freedom. They are the result of the withdrawal

106. Richard Smalbroke, *Reformation Necessary to Prevent Our Ruin*, p. 33.

107. *An Account of the Societies for Reformation of Manners in London and Westminster*, pp. 17–18. It is interesting to note that the love of association extended to the joint-stock companies also. In 1695 there were about 150 such companies in England and Scotland, 85 per cent of which had been formed since 1688: William Robert Scott, *The Constitution and Finance of English . . . Joint-Stock Companies* (Cambridge, England, 1912), *1*, 327–8.

108. A. F. C. Bourdillon, ed., *Voluntary Social Services. Their Place in the Modern State* (London, 1945), p. 1.

of the government from certain important aspects of life, allowing private persons and organizations to take on functions that might have been or had once been functions of the government.[109] G. D. H. Cole believes that the earliest voluntary societies for social services existed in the early 18th century or late 17th.[110] Certainly the societies for reformation were among the earliest. It is clear from their publications that it was not true then, as it is now, that an Englishman with a new enthusiasm immediately bought a notebook and formed a society. Archbishop Sharp thought the reforming societies were "new things." Certainly they differed from earlier societies and organizations. They were not like clubs, congregations, or religious societies. Josiah Woodward's strained efforts to give the societies a pedigree are evidence of their novelty. They were probably the first voluntary groups organized on a national scale and tolerated by the government to step into a vacuum left by the inactivity of Church and State and, in effect, to take over a part of the functions of Church and State.

Therefore the reforming societies, in spite of their failure and collapse, must be considered important in the history of voluntary association and of free institutions. If the existence of such societies is evidence of the extent of freedom in England, the cause of freedom owes a considerable debt to the moral revolution of 1688 which spawned these societies. That the Church and State, in spite of suspicions and objections, allowed the reforming societies to exist and die of their own

109. In our century, and especially since 1945, the pride in these organizations has been mixed with concern for their future. See Miss Bourdillon's book cited above; Roy Lewis and Angus Maude, *The English Middle Classes* (London, 1949), pp. 266–70; Henry A. Mess et al., *Voluntary Social Services since 1918* (London, 1948), pp. 204–13; and *Clubs, Societies, and Democracy*, Political and Economic Planning Broadsheet No. 263, March 21, 1947.

110. G. D. H. Cole, "A Retrospect of the History of Voluntary Social Service," in A. F. C. Bourdillon, *Voluntary Social Services*, p. 11.

accord was an important precedent that encouraged others to form societies. John Wesley was aware of the history of the reforming societies and their failure.[111] In the 1780's William Wilberforce organized some new societies for reformation of manners. He had read Woodward and realized the importance of efficient organization. Furthermore he realized the significance of such societies. "'In our free state,' he maintained, 'it is peculiarly needful to obtain these ends by the agency of some voluntary association; for thus only can those moral principles be guarded, which of old were under the immediate protection of the government.' "[112]

Others in Wilberforce's time and since have seen that voluntary associations were useful not only in guarding moral principles but in influencing the course of politics. Methods of organization and action which the early reformers had had to teach themselves became the methods of the English liberal societies at the time of the French Revolution, of the Anti-Corn Law League, and later still of the Fabian Society. These later groups, seeing the failure of the attempts to reform men directly, sought the improvement of men and manners indirectly through the reformation of political institutions.

There is irony in the history of the societies for reformation of manners. It was ironical that their influence waned long before the desire to reform manners did; that there actually was a reformation of manners for which the societies could take little credit; that later in the 18th century, in spite of the moral improvement of the nation, moralists and reformers again set up the cry that the nation was debauched, that morals were deteriorating, and looked upon the early part of the century as a time of "unspoiled simplicity" and virtue.[113]

111. John Wesley, A Sermon Preached before the Society for Reformation of Manners, p. 4.
112. Robert and Samuel Wilberforce, The Life of William Wilberforce (London, 1838), 1, 130–1.
113. M. Dorothy George, London Life in the XVIIIth Century (New York, 1926), p. 57.